Adoption Healing

Also by Joe Soll

Adoption Healing… a path to recovery (for adoptees), 2000

Adoption Healing Supplement, 2012

with Karen Wilson Buterbaugh as co-author,
Adoption Healing (For women who lost children to adoption) 2003

with Lori Paris as co-author,
Evil Exchange, 2007, *Fatal Flight,* 2010

Adoption Healing

... a path to recovery

Articles, etc.

Joe Soll 조살, LCSW

Please direct all correspondence to:
Joe Soll, LCSW
74 Lakewood Drive
Congers, NY 10920
Email: joesoll@adoptionhealing.com

"Adoption Healing… a path to recovery – Articles, etc."
By Joe Soll LCSW

ISBN – 978-0-615-75608-0

Library of Congress Cataloging-in-Publication Data
Soll, Joe (date)

Includes bibliographical references.

Dedication

To my natural mother,
whoever and wherever she is,
with love,
and to all those who either are or were
Missing In Adoption.

Table of Contents

(Yes, this last one is out of order on purpose)

Author's Notes

---

*"The horrors of war pale beside the loss of a
mother" - Anna Freud   "or child"- JS*

"Tough times don't last. Tough people do!" - Anon

I had not intended to write yet another version of Adoption Healing but so many have asked me to put all the online articles into a book that I have done just that and added a few more articles to boot.

For convenience, I have chosen to use feminine pronouns throughout the book. There are an equal number of men involved in adoption and it is not my intent to exclude them by my use of the feminine pronouns.

I wrote this supplement to Adoption Healing because in the thirteen years since it was originally published...

I've learned new ways of approaching our healing journey, new ways of thinking, new ways of talking to our inner children, new ways to explain the profound nature of the wounds of the separation of mother and child, new ways helping healers understand themselves, new ways of helping those in reunion negotiate these painful and difficult relationships, new ways of guidance towards peace and contentment in our lives.

How have I learned?

I've learned by listening to my clients, the people who attend the support group meetings and healing weekends and nightly chat.

I've learned by reading between the lines of what has been said.
I've learned by paying attention to what has not been said.

I've learned by watching the eyes filled with dread.
I've learned by watching the eyes filled with tears.

I've learned by watching bodies wracked with pain.
I've learned by watching bodies shaking with terror.

I've learned by listening to the soul crying of adoptees and mothers of adoption loss.
I've learned by listening to my internal response to others.

I've learned by reading books written by others.
I've learned by reading the posts on the message boards of Facebook.

I've learned by being in the company of eagles, the brave souls who are willing to face their demons to heal.

This Supplement is a compilation of what I've learned in last thirteen years and written down so that I can help you on your healing journey.

I originally wrote one book for adoptees and one for mothers of adoption loss.

This Supplement to Adoption Healing is not a revision of the original two books so, if you've not read the original Adoption Healing version that applies to you, I suggest you read it before doing the work in the Supplement..
--

While some of the information in the original two books had to be repeated for the Supplement to make sense, most of the information in this Supplement is new, and in addition to, the original Adoption Healing books.

I hope you read the Supplement, do the work in it and that doing so helps you on your journey of recovery. I do inner child work for a few minutes every day. I do it Every Single day and I look at it as maintenance. I hope you will too. A few minutes a day can change your life forever.

For EVER!

Namasté

JS, April 2013

Acknowledgments

"I know now that this healing happens in spirals and
layers and NOT in steps like a ladder." - SARK

I would like to thank the Forget-Me-Not Society of Vancouver,
Canada and Jung Kyung Sook in Norway for having asked me
to write most of these articles, for without their prodding, I'd
not have thought of writing most of them.

The last chapter was inspired by Kyung Sook.

I made most of these into videos which can be seen on my
youtube channel (adoptionhealing.com/AHVideos.shtml)
or my facebook pages.

And finally, my thanks and appreciation to my editor and
long time friend, Celeste Maier for her generosity, dedication
and skill in editing this book.

Part One

Articles

Affirmations and Why They Work

---

*"The terrors of war pale beside the terrors of healing the
loss of the separation of mother and child and those who
do the healing are the bravest people on earth"*

"To have a good relationship with anyone, we have to take care of our
relationship with our inner self first."

What makes affirmations work

When you talk out loud in your head, you are giving your unconscious
mind an instruction, an order to obey. This becomes a message to your
inner child and for her to "obey", your adult self must intellectually
understand and believe anything you tell your inner child, *e.g.*, it wasn't
anything about her that caused her to be given up. If you don't
intellectually believe what you say to your inner child, she won't
believe it either. Only by telling her the truth can you help her see the
truth... the truth that whatever happened to her was not her fault.

Lovability

Say out loud in your head (to your seven-year-old self), "You are
lovable. I know it doesn't feel that way. What happened to you wasn't
your fault. We're okay." Tell her she is lovable often. Give her a hug.
Tell her you love her. Tell her you are on 24 hour call. Do this over
and over, as often as possible. (16 times in a row, every four hours for
a month should produce a very noticeable change. This will take a total
of about 4 minutes a day.)

Anti-panic/Anti-anxiety affirmation

When feeling panicked, look around the room to verify that nothing is happening and then say out loud in your head, "It's not happening now, I know it feels like it but it's not. Relax. Calm down. I am here. We're safe."

To Sleep

After you get in bed, with lights out…

Say out loud in your head, "Dream Power, help me go to sleep now." Say it over and over and over and over and ov….

If you wake up during the night, you may also say, "Dream Power help me go back to sleep." Or, "Dream Power help me continue my last dream." Or, "Dream Power please, no more nightmares."

All of this may seem silly but I talk to DP regularly and it works.

Antidote to Depression

"Sometimes one creates a dynamic impression by saying something, and sometimes one creates as significant an impression by remaining silent" – Dalai Lama

It is very common for those separated by adoption to suffer from depression.

Long ago I was told I had three choices if I was depressed.

Choice number one, Be miserable. I knew how to do that. I was an expert.

Choice number two. Refuse to be depressed. What? How do I do that? Well, say out loud in your head, "I refuse. I flat out refuse to be depressed" Repeat as necessary. I found that sometimes I could make this work.

Choice number three. Enjoy it. Enjoy it? How on earth would I do that? Well, for starters, put on some favorite old clothes, sweater, robe, etc. Make yourself some comfort food. Perhaps home-made chicken soup, or spaghetti or meat balls. Something that you'd like to be given when you don't feel well. Then get a favorite book to read, or put on some special music or watch a favorite movie or video.

Do for yourself what a mommy would do. I found that sometimes I could make this work too.

4

Then I found out about the following:

It takes a lot of real physical energy (brain power) to keep all our pain, anger and sadness contained.
Keeping all these emotions contained wears us down, uses up energy and depresses us.

If we can find a regular outlet for our pain, anger and sadness, we will be able to free up the energy used to keep these emotions inside us.

Our depression will lift.

So what we need to do is the following:

Start an anger list. Write down everything you are angry about, no matter how picayune. Add to it as often as possible

Channel your anger every single day.

 How? By saying out loud in your head, "I'm going to take my anger and use it to..." and fill in the blank with a physical activity that you need to or want to do. Then get up and do that activity. You are not supposed to feel angry or be specific. Just say the words without thinking of what they mean. When you channel your anger this way, your brain will take your negative (anger) energy to do the task and your good energy, the energy you would have used otherwise, is not touched.

Triple pay off. Your good energy is unused, you release some of the energy that you use to keep in anger and you have reduced some of your core anger. If you are angry about something by all means channel as soon as possible but most of the time your channeling will be done while thinking of other things.

By the way, you may need to say, " I'm going to take my anger and use it to get out of this chair" and then say, "I'm going to take my anger and use it to do a specific chore" If you say the words of channeling and keep sitting, no channeling will happen, that is for sure. When you say the channeling words, out loud in your head, they become an order to your unconscious mind and your unconscious mind will obey.

Start a grief list. Write down everything you lost by being separated due to adoption. Add to it as often as possible Journal your feelings, especially your pain, your sadness. Do this daily if possible, even a few minutes will reap rewards. You will be reducing the amount of pain and sadness that is within you and releasing some of the energy you used to keep in your pain and sadness.

Find a group or a chat to go to as often as possible. The more we can say what we feel, the more we are getting out our emotions and the less energy we will be using to keep those feelings in.

Take care of your inner child every day, twice a day, perhaps when you brush your teeth as that is free time.

It will take some time for all of this to gel but my guess is that within a week or two, if you do this work on a daily or semi daily basis, your depression will be drastically reduced

I have not been depressed for over thirty years. I'd like you to be able to join me in this freedom from depression.

I invite you to try.

Blame Game

"Was it you or I who stumbled first?
It does not matter. The one of us who finds
the strength to get up first,must help the other."
— Vera Nazarian,

I hear that there is a whole lot of blaming going on.

We adoptees blame our moms for not keeping us.

Our moms blame us for not understanding what they went through

We blame our moms for being difficult to deal with

Our moms blame us adoptees for being difficult to deal with

Our moms blame themselves for not keeping us

We blame ourselves for screwing up our relationships

Does blaming really fix anything?

Most of US are used to being blamed.

Our moms were blamed and shamed when they got pregnant.

Since children always blame themselves for what happens to them, we adoptees have a 7 year old inner child who blames herself for not being kept.

Those who are used to being blamed usually do two things. They keep blaming themselves and they are quick to blame others.

We need to remember that we are all trauma victims.

The word victim means not responsible so we need to stop blaming each other. (There is a wonderful little book called 'blaming the victim' that you might wish to read)

We need to have empathy for each other instead of animosity.

We are not responsible for the problems we have from our trauma resulting in our PTSD.

We are responsible for working on our problems but that takes time and we need to allow for the fact that some of us can face our pain quicker than others.

We need to remember that trauma is not negotiable

Our moms often have an IC who is very angry at her lost child for being the way she is

We adoptees AWAYS have a 7 year old who is angry at not being kept.

If we have an angry Inner Child, then we look at the world through anger colored glasses and our adult self will NEVER be able to be objective about the person she lost through adoption.

Therefore moms need to help their inner child understand that it is not her lost child's fault that she is the way she is that its' ok to be angry but it's not fair to blame her lost child.

And we adoptees need to help our child understand that it is not her mom's fault that she couldn't keep her, that its' ok to be angry but it's not fair to blame mom.

When we can help our inner children understand all this and stop blaming the person we lost, stop being angry at the person we lost, have total empathy for the person we lost , a victim just like us, we will stop looking through anger colored glasses.

We must remember that just because WE are ready to face our pain, it does not mean that our mother or child is ready. The fact that they do not call or write or answer our attempts at communication does not mean they don't care. It is not rude or disrespectful, it is a sign of their terror of facing the pain of losing you. Terror is not negotiable and we must respect their terror.

Try to remember the you who existed before you started to face your pain. Think about why you didn't do it sooner. Do you remember your terror?

One of my favorite professors said that each of us does exactly on time for us. Our mother or child is doing it exactly on time for them. We must not blame them for being on their own schedule. They have no way to change it. Be patient with them and yourself and do not blame them or yourself

I think there is often one more hidden dynamic. If we can keep blaming the other person, making them BAD, then we devalue them and therefore the loss is not such a big deal. On a conscious level this may work but unconsciously it doesn't diminish our pain at all.

One of the things we must do as part of our campaign to stop blaming is to grieve what we lost. To have a good relationship with anyone, we have to take care of our relationship with our inner self first and then when we do enough grieving for what we lost, we can start to have good relationships with the people we lost.

In the words of John F Kennedy, "Let us not seek to fix the blame for the past. Let us accept our own responsibility for the future."

When we do that, we can stop the blame game, take care of ourselves and be a lot happier.

Coercion and the Single Mother

*Mind control (also known as **brainwashing, thought control**) refers to a process in which a group or individual "systematically uses unethically manipulative methods to persuade others to conform to the wishes of the manipulator(s), often to the detriment of the person being manipulated".[1] The term has been applied to any tactic, psychological or otherwise, which can be seen as subverting an individual's sense of control over their own thinking, behavior, emotions or decision making.*

*To make someone believe something by repeatedly telling them that it is true and **preventing any other information** from reaching them.*

Adoption workers are biased towards adoption.
They have to be, that's how their salaries get paid.

Once involved in a pregnant woman's life, they steer her into adoption especially after introducing potential adoptive parents into her pregnancy, labor and delivery.

So called open adoptions are merely a scam, closing soon after the agreement is signed. In most states, the mother then has no legal recourse to enforce the agreement.

Mothers interred in maternity homes were removed from school, they were forced to live away from their homes, not allowed to work, forced to use first names and last initials only or a false name. They were often barred from contact with their babies' fathers which prevented some potential marriages. They were only allowed to contact those on an approved list. Incoming and outgoing mail was censored. They were not allowed visits from friends. They were given a daily mantra of, "Your baby needs a two parent home and you are not worthy or capable of keeping your baby, you are not worthy of being a mom."

Many mothers were not told they had a right to visit their baby in foster care. Many mothers were not told about welfare or child support to help them keep their baby. Many mothers were not told they had a period of time in which to reclaim their baby. Many mothers were told that their baby was already promised to a married couple, even before giving birth and prior to leaving the maternity home. From what I understand after almost thirty years of counseling and helping mothers whose babies were removed from them, when they were willing and able to parents, these mothers were not abandoning mothers, they were not unloving uncaring mothers. Their youth and vulnerability were used against them.

Many were told they had to pay the bill before they could claim their child. This was used against those who were in maternity homes and not working so they could make a living, which would have helped them keep their babies.

These so-called homes were punitive and institutional. They were nothing more than holding cells for mothers who were brainwashed into believing there was no other option but adoption.

I cannot imagine being in a more terrifying and vulnerable situation than being pregnant and resourceless. These women were so easily brainwashed by those so eager to take their baby and whose living depended on getting a baby to 'sell' to potential adoptive parents.

These mothers were not told of the life-long effects of "surrender", of living life without their child or children. They were not warned about the trauma they would endure, that they would endure a lifetime of Post Traumatic Stress Disorder which caused many not to have subsequent children, which has caused many to have severe depression, which caused them to live a life suffering from disenfranchised grief, a grief not recognized by society.

They gave birth. They had no celebration of a new life, no baby shower, no congratulations from friends or family. Many were not allowed to ever see their baby or to hold or breast-feed their baby. Many were not told the sex of their child or were lied to about the sex of their baby. Their babies were taken as if they had died, in fact many were told their babies had died, yet either way there was no funeral, no support, no comfort whatsoever.

They were left to cope completely alone after being taught by agencies and others to lie about where they had been and why. They were terrorized into silence for decades. They have suffered from nightmares and health disorders.

There are eight million mothers of adoption loss in the United States, many of whom still live in fear of being discovered, having never told anyone about the child they were coerced to surrender. Not even their husbands. Not even their subsequent children. No one!

These mothers need help so they can heal, so they can understand that they had no choice, that they were literally brainwashed, that what was done to them was wrong, unethical, inhumane, that the people who should have helped them instead helped themselves to their newborn. That they had no support from anyone. That they had no choice. That their babies were removed from them simply because they were unmarried and didn't have income or a husband or a family to protect them, to support them.

I believe it is true that the horrors of war pale beside the loss of a baby.

I believe we need to do something to help these women heal.

I believe we must.

Conflict of Two Moms:
An Adoptee's Dilemma

"I don't think avoiding conflict is not caring. " - Shin

Our first moms need to accept that we can love our adoptive moms.

Our adoptive moms need to accept that we can love our first moms.

We adoptees need to accept that we can love both moms.

As adoptees we are usually socialized to believe we can only love one mother, yet we are told we are adopted and that our first mother couldn't or wouldn't keep us or is dead etc. and that is supposed to be the end of it. But it cannot be. Bonding is a physiological and psychological process that begins in the womb and one part of the process is that babies are born loving their mothers. Then how could we not think about them? Why can't we love both of them?

Since to children growing up, their mothers are all powerful goddesses, children believe they know everything. Therefore to an adopted child growing up, if they think about their first mom with love, their adoptive mom will know and get angry and throw them out. The adoptee knows that she lost her first family for some reason and doesn't want to be "re-abandoned" no matter what.

So, the adoptee has to stop thinking about her first mom. To complicate matters, if the adoptee thinks about her adoptive mom with love, her first mom will know and not return. All of the above is usually

14

unconscious but causes a powerful conflict that is impossible to resolve. It gets buried.

Skip forward to adulthood. If the adoptee can overcome the fear of "abandonment" enough to search, the process and hopefully reunion will trigger the conflict of two moms and an inner battle of loyalty will often ensue. If I love this one, that one will "reject" me and vice versa.

To further complicate matters, it's common for our adoptive parents to be terrified we will leave them for our first parents.

Plus:

Our adoptive moms are often jealous of the love we have for our first parents.

Our first moms are often jealous of the love we have for our adoptive parents.

Our adoptive moms are often jealous of the fact that our first moms gave birth to us.

Our first moms are jealous of our adoptive moms because they got to raise us.

And the adoptee is caught in the middle of this very powerful, emotional conflict. For the adoptee, the usually unconscious struggle seems like life and death. If I choose a relationship with my first mom over my adoptive mom, I will surely die. The fear is that terrifying and no logic in the world can get most adoptees past that without help.

Also, most adoptees have rage at their first mom for leaving in the beginning and cannot trust, no matter what they are told, that their first mom won't leave again. It is often, again unconscious, fear of being loved by their first mom that tips the loyalty scales towards their adoptive mom. This is not about whom one loves more but who is safer to one's inner child who is terrified about being left again.

This conflict can be assuaged for the adoptee if she is willing to dig into the conflict with some inner child work.

For the two moms, understanding the adoptee conflict will lessen their confusion and pain.

For all involved, we need to understand that adoptees can love two moms without lessening the love one has for the other.

Fear of Abandonment

In the very depths of our being as adoptees is a core fear, terror really, of being abandoned.

While it's very rare that we were in fact abandoned, our psychological experience when we lost our mothers was of abandonment. That was our initial trauma.

Trauma victims always fear that the trauma will repeat. It happened once, so it will happen again. Our inner child is sure of it so anything that smacks of abandonment sets us off. Major panic or anxiety attacks are frequent and we usually have no conscious clue as to why?

I call it being street-lamped. We can find rejection or abandonment anywhere at any time without being aware of what's happening. Even a smudge on the side of a streetlamp can do it. We can finish a phone call with our best friend and the moment we hang up we start to think, hmm, her voice didn't sound quite right, I wonder if she is angry with me. Then we try to figure out a way to make a check back call… try to find an excuse to call back to make sure she isn't angry with us, isn't ready to abandon us.

We have a wonderful visit with our "Other", the person we lost because of adoption and as soon as we leave, we have a huge panic attack, think we are being abandoned because leaving them seems like it to our inner child. And what if we never see them again? What if they are angry at us? All of this from the initial trauma causing us to be afraid of it repeating. This can happen at the end of a date, going home and thinking they won't want to see us again.

This can happen if we change jobs or move from one home to another.

All of this from our terror of being left, of being abandoned.

This fear of abandonment is usually the reason we were hyperactive as children. We are looking for danger. The danger being abandonment.

Even as adults, we live with a background fear, our inner child always on the lookout for that danger, the repetition of abandonment..

What can we do about this?

Well we need to start with a fact.

We cannot be abandoned. We CAN be left, but not abandoned.

To be truly abandoned one has to be left in a situation or position in which one will not survive such as being placed on a tiny island without food, water, shelter

What happened in the beginning, even though we experienced abandonment psychologically, was not in fact, abandonment. We were not left to die, we were taken care of,

What happened in the beginning cannot happen again because we are not babies any more.

We need to understand this intellectually and then tell this to our inner child until she understands it 100%

Then she can stop being afraid of being abandoned.

We need to recognize that abandoned is not a feeling. Abandonment is an act and if we think someone is 'abandoning' us, we have horrible feelings generated, usually terror, rage, sadness, leading to a huge anxiety or panic attack. All this happens in the blink of an eye.

If we can step back for an instant and think, am I REALLY being abandoned? As soon as we do that and see that we are not being left to die, the panic attack will subside rather quickly.

When we truly own that we can't be abandoned, our inner world changes in a miraculous way.
We can stop being on guard, we can stop walking around afraid of our shadows.

We can stop walking with fear as our partner

We can start walking without fear

We can start to be truly free.

We CAN be free.

Fear of Mommy Love

---

*"**Love** is what we were born with.*
__Fear__ is what we learned here." –Marianne Williamson

Years ago, a 60 year old adopted woman joined my weekly support group meeting. Her first words were, "I want to search for my mom... I know how to deal with "rejection" but what if she accepts me? I don't know if I could handle that." And she started to sob.

What is this really about? Over the years I've heard so many adoptees express, directly or indirectly that they were afraid of being loved, especially by their natural moms. How could this be so? Why would anyone be afraid of being loved by anyone? And by their own mother?

I remember when my own therapist said she loved me. I wanted to crawl inside the couch in terror. Thank God she understood and helped me understand.

We adoptees lost the most sacred and intense love relationship in the world. The reasons why don't matter. What does matter is that we lost what we needed the most both psychologically and physiologically. On some level we always knew it was missing and always longed to have that love.

As a child it would have been easy to "re-connect" and feel it. However, if as an adult I allow myself to feel the love of my mother, I have three (usually unconscious) problems.

1. Recognizing this as an issue can be terrifying in and of itself.

2. If I let myself feel it, I will feel what I always wanted and what was always missing and the pain of that thought can be terrifying. Terrifying as well is the anger that surfaces when I see what I lost. I fear I will either explode in rage or die from the pain.

3. Trauma victims (the loss of the mother/child relationship is a trauma of the highest order) always believe the trauma will repeat so, if I let myself feel it, my mother will leave again and I will die.

This fear of mommy love can sabotage a reunion in the blink of an eye without anyone being aware of what is really going on under the surface. Moreover, if I am afraid to be loved by my own mother, I may well have difficulties letting anyone truly love me.

This is not a message of doom. We can overcome our fears.

My method of doing this kind of work is Inner Child work. (IC)

1. We must help our IC understand that she/he was and is lovable.

2. We must help our IC grieve the loss of the mommy/child relationship.

3. We must help our IC understand that she/he will not die from feeling mommy love, even though it "feels" like it.

4. We need to trust that our mothers will not leave again and that they do not want to experience this trauma again any more than we do.

5. We need to realize that even if our mothers leave again, we will not die. We are not babies anymore; we are adults and will survive. We survived that loss as a baby without any help from anyone so surely we can survive as mature adults.

This work takes time and effort and commitment, however, if we can do the work, we will be more able to let the important people in our lives truly love us and we will come alive in a ways that we never thought possible.

We will be able to live our lives in happy healthy ways.

Spring is here, time for renewal. How about giving yourself this gift of feeling loved?

Finding a Grave

"When your mother dies, the lights go out." - Anon

"There's no tragedy in life like the death of a child.
Things never get back to the way they were." - President Eisenhower

How do we deal with finding a grave?

Remember that you've already experienced the psychological death of your other when you lost her. When you find a grave at the end of your search or your "other" passes away... the initial loss, the initial trauma of separation of mother and child surfaces and one experiences this new loss as another severe trauma.

(For the sake of clarity, I refer to all children of adoption loss as feminine)

Two of the worst losses in the world are the death of a mother or the death of a child. When someone suffers one of these losses, their grief is understood by others, sanctioned by society and they receive comfort and solace from others.

However, our losses are not recognized by society as a whole and the loss of our "other" needs to be grieved... not an easy thing to do under any circumstances. You've already experienced this death when you lost that person the first time, but what happens when we experience this death again?

No other human beings have to experience the death of the same loved one more than once. We have to do it at least three times (In the beginning, at the time of "Fracture" described in the original Adoption Healing, and when we do our grief work) and that is more than enough for any one person to have to experience.

What happens when we find a grave at the end of our search or we have a reunion and our loved one dies... What happens when we experience this death a fourth time?

When one finds a grave at end of her search...

You are hit in the face with this horrible knowledge which means feeling the horrible pain of losing her again, another trauma. The trauma of your initial loss rises up and you have to face not only the pain of the death of your mother or child but the pain of knowing you will never have a reunion. She will never be real to you and you will never get to see or hold or hear or be held by your very own mother, your very own child, never know what her life was like. And, to top it off you have to accept that it's over, your search is complete, your hopes and dreams are shattered.

Your trauma is magnified beyond anything most people ever have to endure. Your friends and family may not understand, may poo poo it and say, "What are you crying about? You didn't even know her!" Well, you sure did know her. You had a relationship with her in the womb at the very least and she's been in your heart ever since, her absence filling your world.

Remember that even if you are unaware of it, babies and mothers love each other at birth. That's how babies come into the world. I suggest you write a letter to your mother or child as part of your grieving work

If at all possible, a trip to the grave would be an important part of your grieving. Bring your letter to the grave site and place it in the ground to be her forever.

When a there is a death after you've met...

You are hit in the face with the horrible pain of losing her again, another trauma. The trauma of your initial loss rises up and you have to face not only the pain of the death of your child or mother the first time, but the pain of knowing it's over. Your child is dead or, your mother is dead. Everyone's worst nightmare. You will never see her again, never get to hold or hear her again. Your trauma is magnified beyond anything most people ever have to endure. Your friends and family may not understand, may poo poo it and say, "What are you crying about? "What's the big deal?", "She wasn't really your child!" or, "She wasn't really your mother!" Well, she was! There is no such thing as an Ex-child or Ex-mother. You had a relationship with her (your mother or your child) and she's been in your heart all her life, her absence filling your world until reunion. And now she is gone! Again! You have a right to grieve and be patient with yourself. Give extra time to your committee of inner children. They will need extra time to grieve as well.

If at all possible, go to the funeral service and go to the cemetery. This will be a very important part of your grieving. Unless you are physically stopped, be there! She is your child or your mother. The rituals at funerals services and grave-side are designed to promote grieving. Also, I suggest you write a letter to her as part of your grieving work. Bring your letter to the grave site and place it in the ground to stay with her always.

No matter what is said, no matter how little comfort we get from others, we need to be aware that the grieving needs to be done on another level. Careful attention and respect must be given to this additional trauma. We need to be patient with ourselves, knowing our grieving process will be longer. More inner child work will be called for and more journaling as well.

Most of all we need to be kind to ourselves and nurture and give comfort to our inner children.

Hug your Inner Child and let her cry with you, comforting her as often as she needs to.

We need to remember that grieving is a process. It takes time. We need to be patient and trust the process.

To Summarize

- losing our loved ones at the beginning was painful enough, finding a grave or having them die after reunion is, in fact, losing them again and grieving is an absolute must.

- making a grieving list, painful as it is to do, will help you process your loss.

- Grieving takes time. Be patient with yourself. We need to cry until we don't need to any more. We may be calm for a while, then have the free floating sadness, then calm again. The cycle will flatten out as long as you take care of your IC and let her cry with you holding her and comforting her as often as she needs to.

I am truly sorry for your loss.

Fitting In

"I thought I was from Mars, not fitting in was like living in hell." - Anon

At one of my weekly support group meetings, Reverend Mark, an adoptee, asked me what I thought "acceptance" meant and how to achieve it.

It made me think of how I was able to find a way to truly fit in.

First, I had to stop thinking of myself as non-human. Just because I had a very different life experience than most people does not mean I am an alien. Just because people do not understand me, does not mean I am a fake. I did a lot of logical thinking and then explained this to my inner child.

As a child, I was put in the wrong movie immediately after my birth. No clue as to the plot or what had transpired before I was in the scene. I had to find a way to adapt to the script laid out by others. As an adult, I was able to see I had choices. Without being in touch with my inner most feelings, I could never know who I truly was or what I truly wanted to do with my life.

So, I went on my mourning journey. I had to cry about everything I had lost. My mother, my relationship with my mother and the special moments I would have had with her. I had to cry about my lost heritage, losing my clan. I had to give up and mourn the magical thinking that one day the nightmare would end and I would be able to start over with my own mother. I had to cry, soul cry actually, until I didn't need to cry anymore. I needed to do this crying with others who understood and who could give me words of comfort, words no one gave me as a child. Crying until one doesn't need to anymore does not mean there is no sadness... it means that the sadness is no long a problem. It's in its proper place with my other life experiences

I had to learn healthy ways of expressing my rage about all that I had grieved for, all that I had lost. I had to express my anger until I didn't need to express it anymore. Expressing anger until one doesn't need to anymore does not mean there is no anger... it means that the anger is no long a problem. It's in its proper place with my other life experiences.

When all this grieving and anger was dealt with, I could start to let people in, start to feel connected. To do that I had to realize that I could not be abandoned so that even if I let someone in and they left, it would be sad but not an abandonment. The inner child work that allowed me to do this allowed me to feel connected to people which allowed me to start to feel connected to the world, to the human race. When I found out through DNA testing that my natural mother was part Asian, I immediately started to learn and speak Korean and Mandarin, even sign my name in both languages. This gave me a connection to my past, the only truth I know about my beginnings and was the final piece I needed to truly fit in. To belong here on earth with others.

28

By doing this grieving, ranting along with the necessary inner child work, I was finally able to enjoy holidays and even my birthday. I came to believe that my mother is with me all the time. I was part of her body and still am and she is part of my body and therefore part of my life. All of this brings me joy, peace and contentment. Finally I feel whole and at one with life.

During this process, I realized that to appreciate what we do have, we need to grieve what we do not have. This will allow us to enjoy Holidays, Birthdays and other events that we now avoid!

One other thing. I came to realize that my strength to face my demons is genetic. The strength to do this work is genetic, our looks, our intelligence, our talents are genetic. All of these blessings are from our natural family. I became proud of my genes and that too, is part of the healing process and part of fitting in.

Finally, I have come to know that given the horror of losing my mother at birth, an unchangeable fact, I cannot imagine doing anything else with my life than I've been doing. I'd change the hand I was dealt at the beginning, but I'd not change how I'm playing it!

This process really works if you work it. I pray you do.

Get Over It!

---

*'To lose someone you love is to alter your life forever. You don't **get over it** because 'it' is the person you loved. The pain stops, there are new people, but the gap never closes. How could it? The particularness of someone who mattered enough to grieve over is not erased by anyone but death. This hole in my heart is in the shape of your loved one and no one else can fit. Why would I want them to?"* – Jeanette Winterson

How many times have we adoptees and moms heard those three words?
When do we hear them?
What has gone on inside us when we hear them?
Why do people say these words to us?
What can we do about it?

Let's start with when do we hear them?

What do we say that precipitates people telling us to "get over it"?
Usually something like, "I'm adopted and I want to find my mom" or
"I lost a baby to adoption and I want to find her" or
 "I'm adopted and I hurt because I lost my mom" or
"I lost a baby to adoption and I am so sad"

Then "they" say, "what's the big deal, Get Over It!"

Ok, now what goes on inside us when we hear, 'Get Over It!' ??

I suspect that for most of us, it brings up anger at being told our feelings don't matter.

And the sadness that we felt about what we said just sits there.
So the anger and sadness have to be stuffed.
Why do people say these words to us?

I think (and I discuss this at length in "Why Don't They Want to Listen?" video) that they don't want to even try to imagine what it would like to have lost a mother or child.

This doesn't make it okay but it might help us deal with it a little better. Knowing it's not about us helps us do the inner child work which will reduce our anger at being dismissed and allow us to comfort our inner child as well, which will help with the buried sadness.

What can we do about it?

Well, what are some of the things we can say in response to being told to "Get Over It!"?

"If you told me that this was the anniversary of your mother's death 40 years ago and you were sad about it, and I told you to get over it, how would you feel?"

"If you told me that this was the anniversary of the day your child was kidnapped 40 years ago and you were sad about it, and I told you to get over it, how would you feel?"

If I don't get an apology after these questions, I think I have to consider whether I want to continue to interact with this person

And I must make sure to tell my committee of inner children that this person's words are about her lack of understanding, not about us and our feelings.

I may want to say to them, Since feelings are never ever wrong, I am always entitled to feel what I feel without criticism."

31

The only way to get over something sad is to walk through it, grieving while doing so.

I am doing exactly that so please never tell me to "Get Over it" again. I'm walking as fast as I can!

Good Grief: Making Sense Out of Suffering

"To weep is to make less the depth of grief." — William Shakespeare

"In times of grief and sorrow I will hold you and rock you
and take your grief and make it my own. When you cry
I cry and when you hurt I hurt." – Nicholas Sparks

The first two words, "Good Grief"can express many things including, surprise, horror and sadness. Our sadness, the loss of what to me is a sacred relationship, is rarely dealt with in a way that will promote healing.

The last four words may cause you to sit up and say, "What? Suffering makes sense?"

Let's explore a bit...

How can we make sense of it? By understanding the causes of the suffering and resolving it.

Resolution means accepting the reality of what happened. We need to recognize how bad our trauma was and do our healing work so that we are not in pain all the time. We must accept our trauma as being as bad as it was, without downplaying it in any way.

In the beginning, when mother and child were separated, each of us experienced the death of the person from whom we were separated. There is no difference in the experience of losing a mother or child to death or adoption. Baby is here, baby is gone. Mommy is here, mommy is gone. We experience that death but what *is* different is how we would be treated if there is a death as opposed to an adoption.

If there is a real death, presumably those close to us will say, "I'm sorry your baby died when she was born, you must be sad, let me comfort you", or "I'm sorry your mother died when you were born, you must be sad, let me comfort you." That encourages good grieving of the tragic loss that society acknowledges.

Every mother of adoption loss that I have ever met was told, one way or the other that she did the noble, selfless, loving thing and to go on with her life making believe it did not happen. Every adoptee I have ever met was told in some way that she or he was Special, Chosen or Lucky (which means they are lucky their mother died for them) and to make believe it didn't happen. These scenarios deny loss and deny the need to grieve. If our loss is denied, to survive the pain, we have to hide from it thru denial or repression.

If one has a tooth ache and applies a topical anesthetic to relieve the pain, the decay that causes the toothache continues unnoticed. If we are not allowed to grieve our losses the hidden pain causes emotional decay. The fact *is* that un-grieved losses paralyze lives. Moreover, the subsequent death of any loved one is unlikely to be grieved in any meaningful way as the fear of the pain of the un-grieved adoption loss is likely to inhibit true grieving.

If we are afraid of the pain of our loss, we are not free, we are enslaved by the emotions of adoption. To be truly happy, have peace and contentment, we must find a way to grieve our adoption losses.

Good Grief of the healing kind involves letting the pain out with those who have experienced the same losses. We need to have validation from those who understand. We need to grieve the loss of the person, the relationship with that person and the special moments we would have had. It is not easy to grieve a relationship that we did not experience but it is possible and necessary. We need to cry until we do not need to cry any more. This does not take a long time at all and the relief is incredible. We discover a new way of life. It's called *Living* and that means living without fear of our own emotions

34

We may think, as I used to, that if we start to cry that we will be unable to stop but the fact is that we *will* be able to stop. We may think, as I used to, that if we start to cry our pain will kill us, that we will be annihilated, but the fact is that we will *not* perish.

I *used* to think the above thoughts until I tried, a little at a time, to let the pain out in a way that was safe for me. When I discovered that I would not cry forever or perish, I became unafraid of my pain. I'm not saying it doesn't hurt, but once unafraid, I could let it out so that I could really do my grieving.

Does this way of dealing with the suffering make sense? I sincerely hope so! Because if it does and you try it, you will discover, as I did, that the injuries caused by separation of mother and child can, in time and with work, be dealt with effectively to the point where the loss will not interfere daily in our lives. Instead, the pain might rear its head a few times a year. We may need to cry--get a hug and perhaps vent our anger--but the pain will pass more quickly each time.

"When we do enough grieving for what we lost, we can start to really enjoy what we have, including holidays and birthdays" - JS

Anais Nin said, "And the day came when the risk to remain closed in a bud became more painful than the risk it took to blossom"

Freedom involves Good Grieving.

Together we can do this.

Good Grief! What a concept.

Her Absence Filled My World

"But the absence of him is everywhere I look. It's like a huge hole has been punched through my chest." — Stephenie Meyer

Recently, one of my clients made me aware of a painting by William Kentridge entitled "Her Absence Filled the World." I googled it, found it on line and it moved me greatly.

It is a black and white scene, desolate, figure standing on a hill, almost at the top, an animal, perhaps a cat at her side, faint shadows of other people off to the side. Through therapy I came to know that on some deep level the absence of my mother was always on my mind, too terrifying to be aware of except for fleeting moments which were then repressed. One member of my support group referred to it as her background sadness.

I now think it is more than that, much more. Just as the world of someone whose loved one is missing in action is constantly aware of their absence, their hearts and minds filled with worry, despair... obsessed with thoughts conscious and unconscious of the missing person, finding it difficult to think of anything else, so too do we who have someone missing in adoption have their absence filling our world.

There is a big difference however. Those who have a loved one missing in action have their concerns acknowledged by society, their friends and relatives. On the other hand, those of us who have someone missing in adoption do not have our losses sanctioned by society. We are encouraged or instructed to "Get Over It" or make believe we do not have anyone missing. This lack of sanction or disenfranchisement of our grief makes it worse.

36

Imagine being in an accident and having a compound fracture of your leg, bone sticking out through the skin. You are taken to the hospital in excruciating pain, put on a bed and forgotten about. No pain killers, no treatment.

What would you feel? Rage at not being tended to? (Which literally makes your physical pain worse.) Feelings of despair, helplessness, sadness? And somewhere in your mind would be the most spoken phrase when someone is dying, "I want my mommy!"

When we adoptees and mothers of adoption loss are not allowed to grieve, do not have any acknowledgment of our pain, anger and sadness, the emotions will seek other outlets. Our inner world is filled with the absence of our other and we have to shut down emotionally to survive. This contributes to what can look like ADD or ADHD. We can lose our basic sense of self. We can lose our ability to experience our emotions. As Kathryn Asper put it in, "The Abandoned Child Within", we may experience ourselves as living in the depths of hell.

HER ABSENCE FILLED THE WORLD

We must acknowledge to ourselves, the enormity of this absence. We must do this in support groups, therapy, chat rooms, journaling. We must find safe ways and places to soul cry about our missing other. Being with enlightened or loving witnesses, those who have had the same experiences, the same losses will help us grieve. We can be validated, comforted with words and perhaps held while we cry. We need to be able to say, scream, yell, "I want my baby!", "I want my mommy" and soul cry as much as and as often as we can until the need subsides.

It takes a long time to grieve but it will be a life time of suffering if we do not.

How To Love Your Inner Child
(or any other child for that matter)

"When you look into your mother's eyes, you know that is the purest love you can find on this earth." — Mitch Albom

Let your inner child look into your eyes and see your love for her

Be there.

Say Yes as often as possible.

Let them bang on pots and pans.

If they are crabby, tell them you love them and it's okay to be crabby.

If they are doing things they shouldn't, tell them you love them and find a fun thing to do together.

Realize how important it is to be a child.

Read books out loud with Joy.

Invent pleasures together.

Remember how really small they are.

Giggle a lot.

Surprise them.

Say no when necessary.

Teach Feelings.

Heal your inner child with love and love and love.

Learn about parenting.

Hug trees together

Make loving a safe thing.

Bake a cake and eat it with no hands

Go find elephants and kiss them.

Plan to build a rocket ship.

Imagine yourself magic.

Make lots of forts with blankets

Let your angel fly.

Reveal your own dreams.

Search out the positive.

Keep the gleam in your eye.

Mail letters to God

Encourage silliness.

Plant Licorice in your garden.

Open up

Stop Yelling. (forever)

Express your love.

Speak Kindly.

Paint their tennis shoes.

Handle with caring.

Remember that children are miraculous!

I'm FINE and I'm Certainly NOT Angry!

"Speak when you are angry and you will make the best speech you will ever regret". - Ambrose Bierce

I've done a workshop at conferences called, "I'm FINE and I'm Certainly NOT Angry".

Each time I've done it, the room has been packed, filled to the brim and at the end, when I ask for questions, there are always one or two who stand up and adamantly say 'but I'm not angry!"

I ask them why they attended the workshop and they look at me with a puzzled look and don't reply.

I suspect that lack of awareness of one's inner most emotions is very common and awareness of anger can be terrifying.

If we are not taught as children how to manage our anger, as adults it can be a formidable chore.

We may fear that we will explode or hurt someone with our anger.

Our fear of fear may keep us unaware that our anger even exists.

It is common for someone to say , "But I KNOW I'm not angry. I'd know if I were!"

In fact this is not so. We all have hidden emotions and if they are hidden, by definition we are unaware of them.

We don't know what we don't know.

However, we may show it passive aggressively. It may show on our face, or in our eyes, in our words.

If we have buried anger, we will likely look at the world through anger colored glasses. and it will show, it will affect our lives, our health and our relationship with those around us.

Why would we have anger in the first place?

To begin with, the loss of a baby or the loss of a mother is a huge trauma and trauma victims usually are angry that it happened.

In addition, we often have those in our lives who tell us we shouldn't BE angry which only makes us angrier.

Anger is not a bad thing, it's necessary part of our life, it's what we do with it that can be a problem.

In the words of Buddha, "Holding on to anger is like grasping a hot coal with the intent of throwing it at someone else; you are the one who gets burned."

I think that the anger from losing our "other" is like the fumes of gasoline in an empty tank one small spark can cause an explosion. We must empty out the tank, fill it with fresh air and then we will not be explosive!

So, how do we empty out that tank?

First we need to acknowledge what's in it.

Once we do that, we can begin.

We can make an anger list. Put everything we can think of on the list, no matter how picayune.

We can journal it until we don't need to any more.

43

We need to express it to those who will validate it for us, until we don't need to any more.

And lastly, we need to channel it. We can use our anger in physical activities.

To channel it, we say out loud in our head, "I'm going to use my anger to clean the house" and then clean the house.

When I say this out loud in my head, it's an order to my unconscious mind.

My unconscious mind will take my negative energy (my anger) and use it to do the chore, leaving the good energy that I would have used otherwise.

(In fact, we can channel anger on a daily basis using any negative energy we have and we will have more and more free energy to live our lives.)

The chore gets done easier and we have less active anger.

Our anger becomes like a banked fire, waiting to be used in an emergency but otherwise quiet,

The more we do these anger exercises, the more our active anger gets put in the basement of our mind, available for emergencies and the less volatile we become.

One day we will be truly be able to say, I'm fine and I'm really not angry!

One day we can become as light and free as the clouds!

Lost Language

"Language exerts hidden power, like the moon on the tides."
- Rita Mae Brown

One of the things I frequently hear from my adoptee clients, reunited or not, is that they do not 'feel' connected to the world or to their family. Erik Erikson, the famous psychotherapist said that if one does not know one's forebears for two generations that one cannot have a sense of actuality. He defined actuality as experiencing one's feelings and events as real. Without this sense of actuality, one cannot feel connected.

Many of my clients are adoptees who were born in other countries. The more information they can get about their country of origin, culture, food, music and language, the greater the opportunity to 'feel' connected and to gain that sense of actuality.

One of the things I recommend is that the adoptees try to learn the language of their country, their "Mother Tongue." I believe the roots of the language are already implanted in their brains. Without a doubt they heard that language in utero and most often heard their language for many months in their country of origin before being brought to the U.S or Canada or elsewhere to be adopted.

If they adoptee is willing, learning their 'root' language is usually easy for them, however there is often great resistance to such learning. After much discussion, what usually is discovered is fear of the almost unbearable pain of connecting, as it makes all the losses of one's natural mother, mother country, mother tongue, mother culture etc. real. This is true and this is necessary for one to heal from these losses..

What I have learned is that to really connect, one must grieve as much as possible of what one lost. I suggest that to do this we must make a grief list, a list of everything lost through adoption and cry about it until we don't need to cry any more. We need to do this slowly, at our own pace. Little by little, we will stop being afraid of the pain and allow ourselves to feel the connection. By doing this healing with inner child work, we will discover that we will be in control of our pain and therefore know that we will survive the process.

When this is done, one will usually be able to learn the language of one's homeland rather easily and be able to feel connected in a wonderful way to one's roots.

Also, I believe that learning our Mother Tongue, the language that we were 'wired' to use from birth can literally enhance our creativity as adults and enhance our overall healing process, enhance our becoming our true self.

I hope you try… after all, what can you lose!

Namasté

Must I Be Grateful?

"We can spend our whole lives escaping from the monsters of our minds" - Pema Chödrön

Last century, at my very first adoption support group meeting, the first thing I learned about was gratitude.

I was so terrified before I went to that meeting that I literally hid in a doorway across the street and waited for someone who looked "safe." A pleasant looking woman approached the entrance so I quickly crossed the street and walked in behind her. It turned out that she was, as far as I know, the first natural mom with whom I had ever spoken.

The meeting began as the feisty group leader stood up, introduced herself and started by asking us to raise our hands if we were grateful. More than half of us put our hands up and the leader said, "Why? Why should any of us adoptees be grateful?" A few spoke up saying they owed it to their adoptive parents for taking them in. A few said they were grateful for being adopted. Most were silent. The leader suggested that we owed nothing for being raised. It was the obligation of our adoptive parents to raise us, give us everything they possibly could to ensure that we were healthy, safe, well fed, clothed, educated, etc.

She said that all children deserved these things and that parents owed it to their children. Some parents may not be able to give it but they do owe it. It is one of the obligations of parenting. In fact, she went on, our adoptive parents should be grateful to us for giving them the chance to raise a child.

Gratitude feeds the belief that we should be people pleasers. Gratitude keeps us subservient to others and keeps us enslaved.

How do we change our built in belief to be grateful?

Well, first we need to believe intellectually that gratitude is not appropriate. Being appreciative for our parents going above and beyond the basics is appropriate, but gratitude is not. Second, we need to tell our inner child that she does not need to be grateful and that she will not be punished if she is not grateful. We need to keep telling her this until she believes it 100%. Third, we need to throw the word out.

Put the "G" word with Special, Chosen and Lucky and with the "R" word, Rejection.

They all belong in the trash can.

Now enjoy the freedom from the need for gratitude.

Prep List for Adoptees Who Are Searching

"By failing to prepare, *you are* preparing *to fail."* — Benjamin Franklin

If one wants to learn how to fly a plane, one takes flying lessons. Ground school first, then flying with an instructor, then when one has enough knowledge to handle anything that happens, one can solo.

If one just hops in a plane, without doing the work, one is likely to crash and burn. One might do well, but the odds are against it.

Preparation for reunion is like taking flying lessons. Ground school involves reading adoption related literature. Going to groups, counseling, chat rooms, talking to other adoptees and moms is your flight time.

If you just jump in without the prep, you might do ok, but the odds are you will sabotage your reunion.

Reunions cannot and do not fix our pain. Reunions always bring up the pain of our losses which is normal and necessary. The better the reunion, the deeper the pain. The pain of our losses, the pain of what we missed.

One must walk through this pain to heal. The rewards of doing this prep work are beyond compare.

From those who have prepared, I have never ever heard, "I wish I had not done this." From those who have not prepared, I often hear, "I wish I had gotten ready before I searched."
From those who prepared, what I usually hear is, "Thank God I was ready!" I pray you prepare!.

"The adult adoptee must walk through the fear which he/she experiences in a search. If he/she does not walk through it, he/she never overcomes it. Those who do not make contact themselves are never released from this fear." - Jean Paton. The first adoptee to search, start a group, write a book about it. The "mother" of the search movement.

(I have a legal and ethical obligation to make sure someone is prepared to search before I help them do that in any way.)

You know you are ready to search when:

You have read and understood "The Girls Who Went Away".

You have talked to other moms and adoptees.

You have read and understood "Primal Wound".

You have read, and understood "Adoption Healing... a path to recovery (for Adoptees)" and done all the exercises.

You have read, and understood "Adoption Healing... a path to recovery (for Moms)" and done all the exercises.

You have read, and understood "Adoption Healing... Supplement and done all the exercises.

You are journaling and channeling your anger daily.

You are talking to your Inner Child daily.

You have done the lovability affirmations and your inner child has told you that she/he is and always was lovable.

Your inner child has told you about her/his rage at mommy for not being kept.

You have convinced your IC that mommy had no choice, that it was not her fault and that it's not fair to be angry at her.

Your IC has said the above to you.

You and your IC know you cannot get rejected when you make contact.

You have grieved the loss of your mom and the relationship you might have had with her.

You understand that you have an obligation to continue a relationship with your mom if she wishes to do so.

You have read and understood the Reunion Guidelines.

You have read and understood the Language of Adoption.

You have written down all the possibilities that you may find and know that no matter what you find, you will be ok.

You have let yourself experience the feelings that would exist for each possibility above.

You have read about genetic attraction and know to be on guard for those feelings so as to not get into a bad situation.

You know that reunions do not fix anything.

Prep List for Moms Who Are Searching

The will to win is nothing without the will to prepare." - Juma Ikangaa

If one wants to learn how to fly a plane, one takes flying lessons. Ground school first, then flying with an instructor, then when one has enough knowledge to handle anything that happens, one can solo.

If one just hops in a plane, without doing the work, one is likely to crash and burn. One might do well, but the odds are against it.

Preparation for reunion is like taking flying lessons. Ground school involves reading adoption related literature. Going to groups, counseling, chat rooms, talking to other adoptees and moms is your flight time.

If you just jump in without the prep, you might do ok, but the odds are you will sabotage your reunion.

Reunions cannot and do not fix our pain. Reunions always bring up the pain of our losses which is normal and necessary. The better the reunion, the deeper the pain. The pain of our losses, the pain of what we missed.

One must walk through this pain to heal. The rewards of doing this prep work are beyond compare.

From those who have prepared, I have never ever heard, "I wish I had not done this." From those who have not prepared, I often hear, "I wish I had gotten ready before I searched."

From those who prepared, what I usually hear is, "Thank God I was ready!" I pray you prepare!.

"A natural mother must walk through the fear which she experiences in a search. If she does not walk through it, she never overcomes it. Those who do not make contact themselves are never released from this fear." - JS

(I have a legal and ethical obligation to make sure someone is prepared to search before I help them do that in any way.)

You know you are ready to search when:

You have read and understood "The Girls Who Went Away".

You have talked to other moms and adoptees.

You have read and understood "Primal Wound".

You have read, and understood "Adoption Healing... a path to recovery (for Moms)" and done all the exercises.

You have read, and understood "Adoption Healing... a path to recovery (for Adoptees)" and done all the exercises.

You are journaling and channeling your anger daily
You are talking to your Inner Child daily.

You have done the lovability affirmations and your inner child has told you that she/he is and always was lovable.

Your inner child has told you about her rage at not being allowed to keep her child.

You have convinced your IC that you had no choice, that it was not her fault.

Your IC has said the above to you.

You and IC know you cannot get rejected when you make contact.

You have grieved the loss of your child and the relationship you might have had with her.

You have read and understood the Reunion Guidelines.

You have read and understood the Language of Adoption.

You understand that you have an obligation to continue a relationship with your child if she wishes to do so.

You have written down all the possibilities that you may find and know that no matter what you find, you will be ok.

You have let yourself experience the feelings that would exist for each possibility above.

You have read about genetic attraction and know to be on guard for those feelings so as to not get into a bad situation.

You know that reunions do not fix anything.

PTSD

"There are wounds that never show on the body that are deeper and more hurtful than anything that bleeds." - Laurell K. Hamilton

"I became what I am today at the age of twelve, on a frigid overcast day in the winter of 1975. I remember the precise moment, crouching behind a crumbling mud wall, peeking into the alley near the frozen creek. That was a long time ago, but it's wrong what they say about the past, I've learned, about how you can bury it. Because the past claws its way out. Looking back now, I realize I have been peeking into that deserted alley for the last twenty-six years." - Khaled Hossein

In layman's terms, what is PTSD and how does it relate to adoption?

PTSD or Post Traumatic Stress Disorder occurs after you've seen or experienced a traumatic event that involved the threat of severe injury or death.

The loss of a mother or child is a severe trauma causing PTSD.

When a mother and child are separated by adoption, they both experience the death of their other. The only difference between the experience of losing a mother or child to death or kidnapping or adoption is the way you are treated.

Mommy is here, mommy is gone. Baby is here, baby is gone. That is a death. That is a trauma. If there is a real death, one is usually treated with respect. When it comes to a psychological death as in adoption loss, one rarely gets treated with respect.

In the words of Anna Freud, "The horrors of war pale beside the loss of a mother." I think that holds true for the loss of a baby. So our adoption losses are a trauma of the highest order, causing PTSD

PTSD changes the body's response to stress. It affects the stress hormones and chemicals that carry information between the nerves.

Our adoption loss symptoms of PTSD fall into three main categories:

1. "Reliving" or fear of reliving the event, which upsets our day to day living

> This means constant fear of abandonment which can be an unconscious fear.
> Background sadness and despair.
> Panic attacks.
> Interpersonal relationship difficulties .
> Lack of self-worth.

The above means:

> Flashback episodes, where the event seems to be happening again and again.
> Repeated upsetting memories of the event.
> Repeated nightmares of the event.
> Self-blame or guilt for the traumatic event.
> Strong, uncomfortable reactions to situations that remind you of the event.

2. Avoidance

> Emotional "numbing," or feeling as though you don't care about anything.
> Feeling detached.

Difficulty trusting others.
For the moms, being unable to remember important aspects of the trauma.

Having a lack of interest in normal activities
Showing and being less aware of your moods.
Avoiding places, people, or thoughts that remind you of the event.
Thinking you are doomed and have no future.

3. Arousal

Difficulty concentrating.

Startling easily.

Having an exaggerated response to things that startle you.

Being more aware of what's going on around you meaning .

Being on the alert for danger.

Feeling irritable or having outbursts of anger.

Having trouble falling or staying asleep.

You might feel guilt about the event (trauma), thinking you caused it somehow.

You might also have some of the following symptoms, which are typical of anxiety, stress, and tension:

Agitation or excitability.
Dizziness.
Fainting.
Feeling your heart beat in your chest.
Headaches.

What can we do to heal?

My preferred method is to work with our inner child.

We need to recognize that losing one's mother or child at birth cannot happen again because we are adults. We need to explain this to our inner child until he or she believes it.

We need to grieve the loss of our other just as we would grieve a real death.

We need to talk about our trauma as much as we can, at our own pace with those with whom we feel comfortable.

We need to respect our fears. Doing this work is usually terrifying, yet the more we do it, the less we will be terrified. It's like dipping your toe in the water bit by bit, getting used to the pain, anger and sadness while knowing it can't happen again.

We must not watch the clock while doing this work. Our healing is like climbing a mountain of recovery. Each person's path up their mountain is windy and full of dips and gullies and crevices that must be traversed to get to the top and get to the top we will!

Keeping in mind that we survived our trauma without support or help as young people and if we could do that alone, we can surely survive the healing with the caring support of those around us as adults.

We can do this! And, as long as we do not give up, we can and we will Heal!!

"Injuries caused by separation of mother and child can, in time and with work, be dealt with effectively to the point where the loss will not interfere daily in our lives. Instead, the pain might rear its head a few times a year. We may need to cry--get a hug and perhaps vent our anger--but the pain will pass more quickly each time."

In the words of Anais Nin, "And the day came when the risk to remain closed in a bud became more painful than the risk it took to blossom"

Let us Blossom!

The Respect That We Need & Deserve

"I'm not concerned with your liking or disliking me... All I ask is that you respect me as a human being." – Jackie Robinson

One of the biggest complaints I hear from other adoptees and mothers whose children were taken by adoption is the lack of respect shown to them by their significant others

Well, what do we want and what do we deserve?

I think we all want our significant others to try to understand what we feel and why

What do we deserve?

I think we deserve absolute respect.

What does this mean?

To me It means accepting that what we say we feel is valid.

Feelings by definition are valid.
Feelings are never wrong.
Feelings just are. If I say the water is too hot, then for me it is too hot. It may not be too hot for you, but for me it is.

If I say I am sad, then I am sad. You may not see something as sad but for me it is. and that is not up for grabs.

I think it is reasonable for me to want you to read some adoption related literature that might help you understand me better.

I think it is reasonable for me to want you to accompany me to a support group meeting to help you understand me.

I do not expect you to know what it's like to have had my experience. I expect and deserve your empathy, understanding, caring and tenderness.

I want to be able to come to you to get a hug and words of comfort when I am in pain.

I do not think that asking for this is unreasonable or too much to ask.

What I do not want is for you to tell me that I should not feel what I feel.

I do not want you to tell me to stop crying.
I do not want you to tell me to get over it.
I do not want you to tell me that you know others who don't feel what I feel.
I do not want you to tell me there is something wrong with me for feeling what I feel.

I do not want you to tell me I am too sensitive

I want you to understand that I have suffered a trauma of the highest order.

I want you to understand that I am trying to heal from this trauma.

I want you to just be there for me, no matter what

Please give me this respect that I deserve.

Reunion and Regression

"The dream of yesterday is the hope of today and the reality of tomorrow." - Kathy Bell, *Regression*

Reunion relationships are often difficult.

One of the things that complicates reunions is that they usually cause regression.

What does this mean?

Well, for example…

When someone has a temper tantrum, they are acting like a two year old and unaware of it.

Actually, for all intents and purposes, they ARE a two year old.

Their 2 year old inner child has taken over their adult body.
You cannot reason with them. You need to wait until the 2 year old gives up control and/or the adult is somehow able to take control.

Having a reunion usually causes similar internal reactions.
Reunions bring us face to face with our losses.

Reunions wake up painful feelings that have been buried for decades.
This awakening can and usually does cause regression.

The separation of mother and child interrupted nature's process of the continuation of the bonding that began in the womb.

When a reunion happens, our mind and body regress and want to continue nature's process.

The mom will usually regress to the age she was when she lost her baby. (Her younger self of that age takes over her adult body.)

(This means she will be trying to give what she didn't get to give and can be smothering from the adoptee's standpoint.)

The adoptee however will most often have her inner child of different ages take over.

One moment she will act 7 years old, the next moment 2, the next 17, the next 5 and so on.

When her inner children take a breather, her adult self will take over and usually have no idea what has transpired or why.

(Depending on the age of the inner child that takes over, the adoptee may be very needy one minute, very loving the next minute or very bitchy the next, with no apparent reason for the change, and no awareness of it either)

So to manage this,the adoptee and the mom need to do some inner child work to lessen the periods of regression.

How do they do this?

They need to find a way to grieve the loss of their relationship with their other at the beginning, when they were separated by adoption.

They need to grieve the loss of their other and the loss of the relationship they would have had with her.

To do that, they need to make a grief list. A list of everything they lost... Their other, the relationship with their other, special days etc..

Perhaps light a memorial candle in honor of the losses. Journal their feelings and find a way to cry. Hold their IC and let her cry in their arms.

I believe that only by crying about the loss of our sacred relationships with our other will we be able to stop trying to get back the relationship that we lost.

Part of the grieving is accepting that what you lost is gone forever.

You can then explain to your inner child that she can't have what she lost. Hold her and let her cry about this.

Your adult self needs to believe it intellectually before your Inner Child will believe it.

You need to explain to her that she can have a relationship with her other without getting what is gone forever.

Your inner child may fight this acceptance tooth and nail but when she does accept it, you will regress less and your relationship will usually do much much better.

I hope you give your relationship this gift.

Routine for Daily Inner Child Work

"Hell, in my opinion, is never finding your true self and never living your own life or knowing who you are." -John Bradshaw

Every morning while you brush your teeth, give your Inner Child a hug, say good morning and tell her you love her. Then ask her how she is feeling. If all is well then continue your day. If she says she is sad or angry etc., ask her why, listen to what she says, validate her feelings and if she needs some talk time, more hugs, more reassurances of safety and love, take the time to give it to her. You can do all this in the time it takes to brush your teeth.

All the above is the same as you should do with any child in your care.

As you go about your day, listen very carefully to the things going on in your head. We all have a continuous narrative in our heads and one of the chores of our healing is learning how to listen to what's being said and identify who is saying it. (Is it your 7 year old self talking or is it your adult self? Is it an Inner Child of a different age?)

When an adult says for example, "I know I shouldn't have that second piece of cake but I will anyway," it's the adult who says I know I shouldn't and one's Inner Child who says I will anyway! If we can learn to listen before we speak or act, identify the age of the voice we hear, we can learn to not let our Inner Child control our actions and our lives.

The more one nurtures any child, and our Inner Child IS a child, the less that child will try to do things she or he should not do to get attention, hugs, reassurances of safety and love. The less we take care of our Inner Child, the more our Inner Child will try to take over and control our actions without our being aware of it.

So, by learning who is talking, we will be more in control of our lives and have a healthier life with healthier relationships as a result.

During the day, channel anger into your physical activities. You should do this without thinking of anger, just say out loud in your head, "I'm going to take my anger and use it to clean or exercise or walk down the long driveway to get the mail," and then immediately do the activity. The activity gets done without stress and you will be using your negative energy to do it, leaving your good energy for other things.

Your 7 year old Inner Child should not live in the house you grew up in. She should be living with you in an imaginary space that you will create for her in a way that pleases her. For example, a petting zoo including a dolphin she can swim with at any time, or a pet tiger. Whatever she wants is what she gets. All the toys, games, movies she wants and access to any fictional character she chooses to spend time with while you do your daily work.

Here and there during the day, I suggest you do a few of the exercises from the wonderfully helpful, "The Complete Idiot's Guide to Zen Living".

Please don't let the title scare you off, this book coupled with Inner Child work is superb.

Take time, as often as possible, to just be present, to just be in the now with your 'self'.

Take time, as often as possible, to just be in the now with your Inner Child.

Every evening, while brushing your teeth, check in with your Inner Child, ask her how she is doing, give her a hug, tell her you love her and wish her sweet dreams. If she needs some extra talk time, give it to her. If she wants to snuggle with you, that's ok too.

If you do all the above, eventually you will both sleep well and wake up refreshed and this will keep you and your Inner Child healthy, peaceful and content.

I hope you take care of your Inner Child this way

It is the way I take care of mine.

Snippets

In private therapy details matter. In a group setting too many details dilute the emotions and are counterproductive. The most effective way of making progress is to make simple feeling sentences such as: "I'm sad I didn't get to be raised by my mum." Or, "I'm angry I was not allowed to raise my child." When done this way, the feelings will not be pushed aside. Here is an example of Less being More.

"We make the past mean different things by what we do with the time that comes after it" - David Milch & Stephen Bochco

If I go to the doctor and say my elbow, knee, tummy, front tooth and toes hurt, Doc will say, "Slow down. Tell me about each individually." "Ok, Doc, my tummy hurts." Doc will say, "How does it hurt? What kind of pain? Be specific. Does it sting, burn, ache, clench?" "It burns, Doc." Doc will say, "When does it burn?" I need to be able to say, "After I eat Thursday dinner." Doc will say, "What do you eat?" I say, "Chili peppers on Thursday evening." So, the best way to start is, "Doc, My tummy burns on Thursday after I have chili peppers for dinner."

This says it all and Doc can now help me. We need to do the same in talking about our emotions. It takes time to learn but we must learn how to do it.

Everyone makes bad decisions some times.

The anger from losing our "other" is like the fumes of gasoline in an empty tank. One small spark can cause an explosion. We must empty out the tank, fill it with fresh air and then we will not be explosive!

When I found out that my mother wanted to see me, "I felt like I found out that there IS a Santa Claus!" - Jane N

One of the things that happens is we grow and those around us who are NOT growing are threatened by us."

"Sometimes there is a lot of rain before the sun comes out"

We don't get to choose what happened to us. We DO get to choose what we do about it!

"I am not what happened to me, I am what I choose to become" -Carl Jung

"Pain Is Inevitable. Suffering is Optional." ~ Zen Saying

"Live your daily life in a way that you never lose yourself. When you are carried away with your worries, fears, cravings, anger, and desire, you run away from yourself and you lose yourself. The practice is always to go back to oneself."

"We only need to do our work and their work will happen in their own time" - Alexsandra

"We are each of us angels with only one wing, and we can only fly by embracing one another." ~Luciano de Crescenzo

Rumi Says... "You were born with wings, why prefer to crawl through life?" I added... "Look behind you and you'll see them firmly attached to your shoulders and recognize that you are flying!"

"The mom connection is like a background OS that is really running the computer but never seen on the screen." - Vati

"A lot of people say they want to get out of pain, and I'm sure that's true, but they aren't willing to make healing a high priority. They aren't willing to look inside to see the source of their pain in order to deal with it." ~ Lindsay Wagner

"There was a mom who attended my group who had been sending her son cards for years with no response. One day, she received a call from her son's girlfriend. She wanted the mom to know that while he was not responding, he had each and every card chronologically saved in a catalogue cabinet."

Time after time, I've had a mom come to my group or me personally for counseling or just call to inquire about the group. The mom says she never wanted her baby that she wasn't coerced, not brainwashed, not in pain. Some moms will say this for years and years. One day, out of the blue, they get into horrible pain (or call years later in horrible pain). While sobbing almost uncontrollably, they will say they all of a sudden remember the day they signed the papers, how they didn't want to do it, how they couldn't find a way to not sign them, how much they wanted to keep their baby. The events surrounding her pregnancy and loss of her baby are repressed (hidden from her conscious memory), to enable her to survive emotionally. Every mom and every adoptee has had some of their experience repressed in order to have survived the trauma. We "wake up" when we are ready. We have no control over WHEN we wake up. Our unconscious mind is in charge of this. This is the same phenomenon as the adoptees who say they are not affected by adoption. I used to tell the same story and I remember how much in the dark I truly was because of the terror of feeling the pain. What all of us must do is deal with our own pain, anger and sadness first. Only then can we look at things with an open mind.. If we look at things through anger colored glasses, we will not be able to be objective.

I heard Rollo May, perhaps the most famous existential psychotherapist of all time, say the following (slightly paraphrased) at an adoption conference in Boston in 1987, "When you make a decision, that decision is based on your age, your life experience, your knowledge, your wisdom, your childhood and the influence of those around you. At the moment you make that decision, you have NO other choice."

If one can hold unto the belief that one's mom did not care enough to keep her or that one's child does not care enough to have contact, then the mom or the adoptee is being devalued. Devaluing them means that one didn't lose so much and therefore lessens the pain. However, this only reduces pain on the surface. Way down deep, thinking we were not or are not loved makes it worse. We need to stop thinking we know what went on or goes on inside of our "other" and remember that we've all suffered what, in the words of Anna Freud, makes the horrors of war pale in comparison. Each of us will face our pain when we are able to do so. Our terror rules our unconscious mind. We need to keep this in mind and find total empathy for our "others" if we want to heal and find peace.

In the words of Clarissa Pinkola Estés, in Tales for the Abandoned, those who have been abandoned (and we all have experienced it) and work it through (do their healing) ARE the strongest people on the face of the earth. Believe it!

Holding on to anger is like grasping a hot coal with the intent of throwing it at someone else; you are the one who gets burned. ~Buddha

"Holding a grudge is like drinking poison and waiting for the other person to die."

"Be who you are, say what you feel. Those who matter, don't mind. Those who mind, don't matter." --Dr. Seuss

Let no one deceive another or despise anyone anywhere, or through anger or irritation wish for another to suffer" - Buddha

"When it comes down to it, we are not allowed to know our "other" because it might upset someone."

"Warriors confront the evil that most people refuse to acknowledge" - Bohdi Sanders

"Food for thought: Pain is our friend, truly... without pain, we'd be dead. Pain shows us the path we must take... pain helps us heal and without it we'd not know where to put the emotional bandages!" - JS

Special, Chosen and Lucky

"Why is it I just don't belong? Why is it I just don't fit in,
fit in with anyone, any place? Why is it so?
When I look around, I've no place to go.
Why is it I don't feel related to most familiar scenes I see?
I wonder why was I created to be me, only me?

Why is it I feel so alone? Why is it I feel so left out,
left out of everything, anything I want to do?
Seems false and unreal, Is anything true?
Can't get into nobody's head, nobody's thoughts, are matching mine!
When I need sun, it rains instead! Why can't my day be fine?

Why is it I just don't belong?
Why is it I just don't belong?
Why is it everything goes wrong?
When all I want, all I want,
All I want, is just to belong! " – Gene Bone & Howard Fenton

Special, Chosen and Lucky. How many times do we adoptees hear those three words? They are presumably said with all good intentions, what goes on inside us when we hear them?

If I am special, do I have to follow the rules?

If I am chosen, did I come from a baby supermarket? Why did they pick me?

If I am lucky, what makes me so?

If I am special, why was I available to be chosen?

If I was chosen, did someone unchoose me first?

If I am lucky, why do I hurt so much inside?

If I am special, why does it not feel good when I hear it?

If I am chosen, who were the other contestants?

If am lucky, does that mean my first family was "bad" in some way?

Each time someone says either of those words, it is a reminder that we are adopted. The intent is to make us feel good, not hurt, not think about our natural mothers. Yet each time we hear these words, how can we not on some level think of where we came from? It's like telling us to not think of pink elephants. Each time we hear the words it causes us internal pain. We may not be conscious of it, but it has to be there.

The reason why we adoptees do so much day-dreaming (which to the uninformed mental health professionals looks like ADD) is because we are constantly (at least unconsciously) trying to figure it all out. Who and why are the biggest unanswered questions and our minds struggle to understand what no one can or will tell us.

There are phobic and counterphobic reactions to pain and fear. The phobic adoptee tells no one they are adopted. The counterphobe flaunts being adopted, tells others how special she or he is.

In reality, the loss of our mothers at birth was a trauma of the highest order that is worse than the horrors of war. (Anna Freud) Each time we hear those three words, that trauma is stirred up. When we are separated from our mothers we experience their death. There is no difference in losing a mother to death or adoption. Mommy is here, mommy is gone. Poof! Death as far as the infant's experience goes.

If we are special, does that mean it is good to lose a mom?

If we are chosen, does that mean our parents took us from our mothers on purpose?

If we are lucky, does that mean we are lucky our mothers are dead for us?

I like to throw away words that hurt, like the "R" word... Rejection

Maybe we should throw these three words away as well. Spread the word, throw out "S", "C" and "L" because they are not what they say they are.

Terror is Non-negotiable!

---

*"Death has but one **terror**, that it has no tomorrow."* – Eric Hoffer

Terror is Non-negotiable!

Why am I saying this?

Well, first a few questions…

Why do some adoptees and moms have so many walls up?
Why can't they tell us they have walls up?
Why do they seem so cold and distant?
Does it mean they don't care?
Is their behavior disrespectful?

I think the answer to all the above is terror, non-negotiable terror.

Trauma victims always fear the trauma will repeat. The unconscious mind says, it happened once, it WILL happen again.

Reunion, or the thought of reunion brings one consciously or unconsciously to the feelings of the initial trauma, separation of mother and child.

Some people can manage to face their fear and some cannot. It is not about choice. Those who cannot face their fear have what is called fear of fear.

Their terror is so severe that they believe they will be instantly annihilated if they even think about being afraid... they are so afraid of our their fear that they become completely unaware of it.

Thus, when the person with whom you are in reunion or with whom you wish to be in reunion avoids talking about adoption related feelings, or insists they are okay with adoption or do not refer to you as their mother or child or insist they don't hurt, or have no anger or sadness, it is likely that they are terrified of their emotions and unaware of the terror.

For example, one's "other" may not be able to acknowledge being one's child or one's mother but that does not mean they don't believe it. It means that acknowledging the connection will bring the feelings of the loss with it, the profound pain of the wounds of separation and that terrifies her.

Some of us wake up earlier than others in terms of getting help. There is no time table for when this happens and we must not blame those who are still sleeping.

If one believes in primal wound theory, then one knows that no one can lose a mother and not have extreme pain, anger and sadness about it. Nor, in my opinion, can a woman lose a child and not have extreme pain, anger and sadness.

When someone IS terrified of annihilation and is unaware of the terror, that terror is non-negotiable.

Only when the person can safely become aware of their fear can they begin to face it and tame it.

Until then, their unconscious mind is at battle stations. All their walls up and they are unapproachable in terms of being open to discussion.

The tendency is for the recipient of the distancing to believe that they are being rejected, snubbed, unloved, uncared for, or disrespected. They become sad and angry. They blame the one who has their walls up.

It is vital that we do not blame our "other". It is very important to understand that the walled up person is not consciously choosing to be distant. Terror is the likely cause and therefore non-negotiable.

We must remember that all of us who have been separated by adoption suffer greatly. Being awake is not a function of more or less pain. Some of us are lighter sleepers than others.

We need to be patient with the sleepers. We must not take their distancing personally. If we can do some good inner child work, convince our inner core that the way we are being treated is not about us, is only about the terror of our other, we will be sad but it won't hurt the same way at all.

Someone who is terrified can be viewed as what Clarissa Pinkola Estés refers to as a "Stone Child"... Someone in so much pain, bent over, hugging themselves and yet if approached by anyone offering comfort they scream, "Get the hell away from me!"

We must not blame the sleepers. We need to have empathy for the "Stone Children."

We need to take care of our own pain first. Like they say on a plane before takeoff, if there is an emergency put on your Oxygen mask first.

We have to do our healing first or we won't be able to be there for anyone else, including our other when they wake up. When we take care of own healing, we will communicate with others in a way that is more likely to be receptive.

All of us have our own reactions to our trauma. None of us want to be blamed for the way we are,

Let's not blame our "others" for being the way they are.

The 'R' Word

---

*"Most of us can find rejection anywhere at any time,
even a smudge on the side of a streetlamp."*- JS

When facilitating my support groups or nightly chat or in a session with one of my clients, I often hear someone say that they are afraid of getting "rejected" again. This is referring to what might happen if one searches and gets turned down, or if a reunion goes awry.

As adoptees, what we need to understand is that we were not "rejected" when we lost our mothers. We need to understand that all babies are lovable, without exception and therefore, no matter what happened it was not rejection. For me to be rejected there has to be something about me that is not likeable, not lovable. Since all babies are lovable then I could not have been rejected. If a mother, for some reason does not love her baby, that is about the mom. It cannot be about her baby, so it cannot be rejection.

The pain of adoption loss is just as profound for a mom as it is for an adoptee. We all survive our losses by pushing them away. When a mom is contacted, the hidden feelings of pain, anger and sadness start knocking at her consciousness. If she cannot face her hidden feelings because they are so terrifying then she may not be able agree to contact.

When someone is truly terrified they usually do not have the ability to confront their fears. This works both ways and we need to respect the feelings of someone who is truly terrified that their feelings will destroy them.

If I choose to search and when I make contact, I am turned down by my mother (or in the case of a mom searching turned down by the child she lost to adoption), that is not rejection of me but an unwillingness of the person found to face her pain. It cannot be about the searcher because the searcher is unknown to the person found. Aside from the terror of facing her pain, a mom might fear severe consequences from her family members who may not know her secret.

Now comes the Inner Child work. What we think, affects how we feel. The words I say about myself, the words I think about myself, greatly affect my emotions. If I can stop thinking the R word, if I can remove the word "Rejection" from my vocabulary, I can do what I want with impunity because I know that: #1 I was not rejected at birth, #2, I cannot get rejected if I should choose to search for my family. I can get told "No" and that would be sad, but it would not be devastating because it would not be "rejection" of me.

No matter what we do, being told "No" will be horribly sad and hurt like hell. However, if I've done my Inner Child work, in the end, I will know that it's not a 'rejection' of me, that it's not about me at all. I will know that it's about the other party's own experience and feelings. My knowing that is what makes the difference. Part of the preparation for search is to be aware of all the things that can happen, both good and bad. If we do this preparation along with the inner child work, no matter what happens, we will be ok. Yes, we may hurt like hell but we will be ok.

I often hear, "I feel rejected, or I feel abandoned." To be clear, abandonment and rejection are not feelings. They are thoughts based on our past experience, thoughts that create great anguish. If we can recognize this and do the thought changing work of this "chapter of our healing", we will remove a lot of anguish from our lives. If I hear myself thinking, "I am being rejected" and stop a moment and ponder.. "Am I being rejected? Am I being abandoned?" I will usually see that neither of those thoughts is true. Also, adults can't be abandoned. To truly be abandoned, one has to be left in a position from which she cannot survive. I suspect that none of us need to worry about that happening. Yes, someone can leave us and that would be sad, but it's not abandonment. Usually these thoughts are the thoughts of our Inner Child so we immediately need to go to our Inner Child and reassure her that what she fears is not happening and cannot happen.

As trauma victims our inner core expects the past to repeat. As adults, we need to be aware that what happened at the beginning cannot possibly repeat as we are adults now and in charge of our lives.

For us to do the above, the first step is to intellectually know that all babies are lovable and then make sure our inner child owns this fact.

Next we have to do the intellectual work of knowing that we were not rejected at the beginning and then make sure that our Inner Child knows that he/she was not rejected at the beginning.

Then, as adoptees or mothers of adoption loss, we have to intellectually understand that we cannot get rejected if we search and then make sure our Inner Child knows that.

The Inner Child work I refer to consists of our "talking" out loud in our head to our seven year old self (for an adoptee) or to the young woman you were when you lost your baby (for the moms) and telling her the intellectual truth that it was not rejection in the past and cannot be rejection now. To do this, we have to have previously done the work of helping our Inner Child know that she was not responsible and was lovable and still is.

If we do this, we will be at a place to never fear losing a relationship ever again. Sure, it is sad to lose relationships, but when one knows it cannot be a second rejection, one is free of one of the biggest adoption issues we all face. I'm not saying this is easy. It takes a lot time and a lot of work but the payoff is a wonderful reward.

Please do me a favor. Throw out the "R" word. It will change your life.

Who's in Charge?

"The closest to being in control *we will ever be is in that moment that we realize we're not"* - Brian Kessler

I was recently asked, "In a reunion, who controls/rules it? The adoptee or the mother?" I believe that if we deem one person to be in control or in charge of, or to rule a relationship, then the other person is out of control or being "ruled" which means they are not free. One person is in a position of "power" or in charge and the other person is powerless, perhaps even infantilized.

I do not think any healthy relationship can exist under these conditions.

Let's substitute "space" for "control" as I think it's a healthier way to look at it. We need to give "space" to the person who is unable to face the painful emotions of reunion. Reunions always cause regression on some level. Aware of it or more commonly not, moms regress to the emotional age they were when they lost their baby. The regression of adoptees however is very dynamic: The adoptee's emotional age fluctuates from 2 days old to 2 years to 7 years to adolescence to adulthood in the blink of an eye, back and forth like a ping-pong ball.

Since those in regression are rarely aware of it unless it's pointed out to them and since reunions bring up all the feelings of pain, anger and sadness of the initial trauma, it may be that one or both of the parties cannot face the emotions that are running rampant through their mind and body. Whichever one of the pair is most afraid of their feelings is the one who must be given the most space... time to realize that these terrifying emotions will not, in fact, kill.

What must not happen is blaming of the other for not being ready to feel the feelings.

Even if that inability happens after reunion as much as a year or more later

Terror is not negotiable. We cannot expect someone who is terrified of their emotions to stop being afraid, just because we love them or want them to or are frustrated with their lack of participation. A mom may not accept being acknowledged as mom. An adoptee may not be able to accept being called a son or daughter.

The terror of recognizing that one's "other" is in fact their lost mother or child makes the loss real which brings up the pain that is lurking below the surface of one's consciousness. Those who experience the terror are experiencing the threat of dying on the spot... re-experiencing the death of their other.

We all experienced the death of our other when we lost them to adoption and are, consciously or unconsciously, terrified we will die if we experience that death again.

No one must rule, no one must control, no one must be in charge. The one who is the most afraid has to be given the most space by the one who is least afraid. We have all suffered a huge trauma. We all suffer the pain of the loss of the mother/child relationship. No one hurts more than anyone else and no one suffers more than anyone else. No one's pain is worse than anyone else. Our pain may at times be different, we all respond in a different way, but no one rules. No one is in charge or in control.

What we must not do is blame our "other"... We all are coming from different life experiences and we must have empathy and compassion for one another.

84

What we must do is throw out the words, "Control" and "Rule" and put them alongside the other "R" word, "Rejection", where they belong.

In fact, the only thing that must rule is Compassion for our other.

What's In A Name?

"What's in a name? That is what we ask ourselves in childhood when we write the name that we are told is ours." — James Joyce, *Ulysses*

We adoptees often go through life using our adopted name without any idea that we might have had an original name.

If we decide to search one of the first things we do is try to get information on our mothers.

This leads us to the fact that we had another name. A different surname, and maybe an original first name. Or that we didn't have a different first name. Why didn't she name me? That hurts. We think our moms didn't care. We have no way of knowing that our moms might not have been allowed to name us. We have no way of knowing if she had a name picked out that she was not allowed to use.

I may think that the name I've been using is not my real name. No wonder it felt weird all my life. Why didn't my adoptive parents keep my original name? Why did they change it? That hurts. I may have an ethnic name, one that is clearly from an Italian family for example and then discover that my real name is from an Irish family. I thought I was Italian. Now I am Irish. I am so confused. I am sad I missed out on my Irish heritage. I am angry I was deceived, even if it was not on purpose.

What about those from another country who grow up being called Rachel and find out their name was Eun Sook? What confusion to look in the mirror in the morning and see an Asian face with a Jewish first name. Who am I really? Am I Caucasian? Am I Jewish when to be Jewish your mother has to be Jewish? People look at me funny when I say my name. It hurts.

Our names are part of who we are and to not know causes pain. If I find my original name that stirs up the pain of losing my first family.

If I accept that I really had a different name, then who am I really? My world is turned upside down. I need to turn it right side up.

To turn it right side up, I need to look at the truth, accept the fact that I had an original name and work through the emotions that are stirred up. Running from the truth only causes the inner turmoil to fester and never be resolved. Dealing with the truth will always help us heal.

Finally, I know many adoptees who took back their complete original names. For most of them, if they worked on their inner feelings first, did some good old fashioned inner child work, it gave them a sense of reality. Their names fit and **they** fit inside their skin in a way they never had before.

Why Are We All NOT Schizophrenic?

"If you talk to God, you are praying; If God talks to you, you have schizophrenia." – Thomas Szasz

"Schizophrenia is usually characterized by withdrawal from reality, illogical patterns of thinking, delusions, hallucinations, and other emotional problems."

I've been asked, "How is it that all adoptees and mothers of adoption loss are not schizophrenic?"

Many years ago, a psychiatrist asked me to consult with her about one of her patients who was an adoptee.

I spent about an hour explaining the wounds of separation of mother and child, the trauma, Post Traumatic Stress Disorder and the profound effects separation has on our later lives.

She had tears in her eyes when she asked me, "How is it that you are all **not** schizophrenics?"

At that time, I had no answer as I had never thought about it. So, let's think about it now.

We adoptees are told we have another mother, and then we are told to forget about her.

Our mothers give birth to a baby, who is taken away   and then they are told to forget about her

Is it not crazy to ask someone to do this? To pretend that something that happened did **not** happen?

Is it not crazy to be asked to create a false reality?

Does it make your head spin?

Is it enough to make you want to pull the hair out of your head?

Is it not like being told to think up is down and down is up?

Is all of this *not* crazy?

Is it not insane?

Is not all of this, Just Plain Nuts?

We have the enormous pain of our losses which we are not allowed to deal with, which we are supposed to bury.

And to survive, we Must bury it.

So, why are we not crazy? Why did we not become schizophrenic?

To me there is only one answer.

Some of us have such a strong core self that we stayed sane in spite of the demands to forget reality.

Some of us have such a strong core self that we stayed sane in spite of the pain, in spite of the total insanity of the situation.

Some of us have such a strong core self that we stayed sane in spite of the demand for us to make believe that what happened to us did not happen.

We were born with that core strength. One cannot develop it. One has it or one does not. We may not be aware of or able to find and use that strength until later in life but once we find it, I believe we are invincible. I believe that those of us who find that we HAVE that strength can survive anything.

We are facing our demons and only the super strong do that.

Only the super strong stay sane in the face of insanity.

Think about what you have survived. Think about the strength it takes to face your demons.

Really think about it.

Is there *Really* anything you can't survive?

Why Don't They Want to Listen to Us?

"They won't listen. Do you know why? Because they have certain fixed notions about the past. Any change would be blasphemy in their eyes, even if it were the truth. They don't want the truth; they want their traditions." - Isaac Asimov

When I graduated from shrink school in 1990, I wrote letters to all the graduate schools in the New York Metro area suggesting that adoption issues need to be taught to all students as a core course or at least as an elective. I received no responses at all. I went to the Dean of my school and asked her about my teaching such a course. She hemmed and hawed, avoiding my eyes. I pressed and she finally told me that there were a lot of trustees and faculty who were adoptive parents and if such a course were taught it would mean there was something wrong with adoption and the adoptive parent trustees would stop helping the university with their funding efforts. To my knowledge no university in the U.S. or Canada teaches adoption issues yet, here in the U.S., adoptees, adoptive parents, natural parents and all four sets of Grandparents comprise about 100 million people which is about 30% of our population. And this figure does not take into account any siblings. The societal hype trumps the truth.

Adoption is glorified in the media. To say anything negative about adoption is looked at as subversive, anti-societal. Those adoptees and moms who are still in denial, and I think they are in the majority, praise adoption, talk about how wonderful it is. Their voices are the ones most heard and promote the societal belief that adoption is wonderful and causes no trauma, no pain.

I think there is something else that keeps so many of us who have suffered adoption loss in denial.

A few years ago, I had an AHA moment. I had just arrived at the local mall when an ambulette pulled in. A dozen or so children got out, all palsied, all in wheel chairs. I took one look and I wanted to run. Inside myself I felt panic, said my anti-panic affirmation, did NOT run, walked inside the mall and took a seat to reflect. Why did I want to run? The answer from within was clear. I could not and did not want to imagine what it would be like to be one of those children.

The thought was terrifying but revealing. Maybe this is the reason so many of us are in denial. The truth of what happened to us is too terrifying to contemplate. Maybe this is the reason other people don't want to listen to us. Perhaps they cannot, don't want to imagine what it's like to have suffered our loss.

When one of us who are aware speaks out, we are looked at as a bit off, an anomaly. I was once on a Sally Jesse Raphael Show and another one of the guests was a social worker who said, "Any adoptee who searches is mentally ill!" I was appalled and tried to argue the point but Sally loved what the social worker said and shut me down.

When we can talk in numbers, when enough of us can find a way to speak out in ways that other people will listen to, we can make a difference. If each of us wrote letters to the editor to our local newspapers on a regular basis, if each of us contacted our local legislators and told them our stories, if each of us told everyone we come in contact with our truth, things would eventually be different.

What does it take for us to speak out?

We may be terrified of the exposure, the shame of being adopted, or the shame of being a mother who lost a child to adoption. If we are afraid and do some inner child work and/or discuss this in our support groups, we can learn that there is nothing wrong with us. In fact, we can learn to be proud that we are strong enough to speak out, that no one can hurt us unless we let them. We can learn that it IS safe to speak out, to tell our truth.

What can we gain individually by speaking out?

Each time we tell our story, we are healing a bit more.

Each time we tell our story and nothing bad happens to us, we are proving to our inner core that it's safe to do so and we are getting in touch with more of our core strength, the strength that helped us survive our trauma.

Each time we tell our story we are on the way to being proud because, in doing so, we are facing our demons and only the bravest of the brave face their demons.

Each time we tell our story we are educating someone who might turn around and educate someone else.

Each time we tell our story to another person who suffered adoption trauma, we are giving them a gift that, if they unwrap it, may help them begin their healing journey.

Each time we tell our story we are, hopefully doing something that may help others join our efforts to make societal change.

In the words of Margaret Mead, "Never doubt that a small group of thoughtful, committed citizens can change the world. Indeed, it is the only thing that ever has."

One thing is for sure. If we do not speak out, if we do not try, nothing will ever change.

In The Company of Eagles

"The warrior looked at the Eagle and saw
The symbol of courage and fierce pride
Whose sacred feather he wore." - Anon

It is very difficult for Trauma survivors to look at themselves as strong, yet what does survival mean if not strength?

How could we possibly have survived if didn't have the strength to survive what I think of as a personal holocaust?

The strength to survive what Anna Freud said was worse than the horrors of war?

Those who face their demons are brave souls indeed! And are we who dare to examine the thoughts and feelings of our trauma NOT facing our demons?

How can it not be brave to touch feelings that have terrified us for so long?

How can it not be brave to do what so many others tell us not to do because it terrifies THEM?

Where do we get this strength? We are born with it, it is genetic. We are all born with a certain amount of core strength. Some have barely enough to manage in this very difficult world. Some have enough to fair well. And we, we have an extraordinary amount. The proof is that we have enough to survive and the extra to do the painful work of healing.

I think of it as emotional root canal. It can hurt like hell and it takes time to be processed. But then healing is possible. And we have the strength to do just that, Heal!

Although it's rare that an adoptee is truly abandoned, our experience IS of abandonment and I think our moms were abandoned by those around them.

Clarissa Pinkola Estés has said that those who have been abandoned and do their healing work ARE the strongest people on the face of the earth.

Believe it, we ARE!

and as such we are all Eagles, brave warriors doing what we have to do.

So, I think of it this way, each of us is in the company of eagles.

I honor the brave spirit within each of you.

I am proud to stand in this company of eagles with you!

Namasté

Part Two

Appendices

"It may be too late to have a good beginning but
it's never too late to have a good ending." - Anon

Appendix A:

Headaches and Acupressure

Over 30 years ago, a Chinese physician showed me how to relieve headaches without medicine.

A simple way using Accupressure that I've been using ever since. I've not had to take a headache med since that time.

Set a timer for 3 minutes or count to 180 in your head once your eyes are closed.

Put your hands in front of you and hold your palms and fingers together, elbows to the side, arms in front of you, parallel to the ground.

Separate the heel of your palms slightly and only have the 1st pads of your fingertips touching slightly.

Take a slow deep breath and let it out slowly

Close your eyes, say the word "relax" out loud in your head. Imagine that your headache travels down the back of your head, down your neck, across your shoulders, down your arms, around your elbows and out through your fingers.

When the timer goes off or you have counted to 180, slowly open your eyes, slowly take your hands apart.

Take a slow deep breath and let it out slowly.

Your headache should slowly subside!

Appendix B:

The Invitation by Oriah Mountain Dreamer, Indian Elder

by Oriah Mountain Dreamer, Indian Elder

It doesn't interest me what you do for a living. I want to know what you ache for, and if you dare to dream of meeting your hearts longing.

It doesn't interest me how old you are. I want to know if you will risk looking like a fool for love, for your dreams, for the adventure of being alive.

It doesn't interest me what planets are squaring your moon. I want to know if you have touched the center of your own sorrow, if you have been opened by life's betrayals, or have become shriveled and closed from fear of further pain.

I want to know if you can sit with pain, mine or your own, without moving to hide it or fade it or fix it. I want to know if you can be with joy, mine or your own; if you can dance with wildness and let the ecstasy fill you to the tips of your fingers and toes without cautioning us to be careful, be realistic, or to remember the limitations of being human.

It doesn't interest me if the story you are telling me is true, I want to know if you can disappoint another to be true to yourself. if you can bear the accusation of betrayal and not betray your own soul.

I want to know if you can be faithful and therefore trustworthy. I want to know if you can see beauty, even when it is not pretty every day, and if you can source your life from its presence.

I want to know if you can live with failure, yours or mine, and still stand on the edge of a lake and shout to the silver of the full moon, "Yes!"

It doesn't interest me to know where you live or how much money you have. I want to know if you can get up after the night of grief and despair, weary and bruised to the bone, and do what needs to be done for the children.

It doesn't interest me who you are, or how you came to be here- I want to know if you will stand in the center of the fire with me and not shrink back.

It doesn't interest me where or what or with whom you have studied I want to know what sustains you from the inside when all else falls away. I want to know if you can be alone with yourself, and if you truly like the company you keep in the empty moments.

May 1994

Oriah Mountain Dreamer
© 1995 by Oriah House, From "Dreams Of Desire"

Appendix C:

Guidelines for Adoption Reunions

*Some of these guidelines for reunion are originally from
Truth Seekers in Adoption in Chicago.
Additions have been made along the way via the Internet*

These guidelines are not cast in stone!

0. Nobody knows the "rules", especially the person who is found.

1. Adoptees may "back off" even if they did the search.

2. Mothers reuniting with their child may not "back off" - especially if they searched.

3. Everyone needs "space", but not endless space.

SPACE means:

Separation
Patience
Acknowledgement
Concern
Empathy

4. For those "in space", a simple card signed "Happy Birthday" or "Thinking of You", are acceptable: this can go on for YEARS, so do *not* have "great expectations".

5. SLOW is the signal especially at the outset.

6. Do not launch into long or angry letters before meeting.

7. Not everything is adoption/reunion related, but separation at birth is a core issue that radiates through almost everything else.

8. Expect that an adoptee will express anger, somehow, some way, probably not overtly, possibly not even recognizing that he or she is angry.

9. When reunion is new, talk to one another about the boundaries you need to establish. (Again, the adoptee has leeway, but the mother must remain in the "responsible adult" role.)

10. Join a support group. Sharing and learning with others is most important.

11. Start your own grief work. Seek professional help if needed.

12 Help your current family and friends to understand that search and reunion will be your "life focus" for a while. Share that you may need a supportive shoulder or open ears. "Advice" may not be heard! Remember that your friends may not understand.. Even you may not understand.

13. Search and reunion are as much about YOU as they are about finding someone. Expect to change in many ways. Do not expect or allow a well-meaning family to expect that search will "fix" you.

14. Remember that real life is "messy", unlike fantasy, which you can bend to suit you. If you aren't ready for "real" and ready to give up fantasies; don't search! And certainly don't make contact!

15. Relatives happen! Relationships take time and work to put into proper perspective. (Remember this when experiencing Genetic Attraction, too!)

16. Family is, ideally, supposed to be fun, thought-provoking, and supportive of each other, while still respectful of independence.

Appendix D:

Important Information re: Searching

0. Preparation in advance is mandatory.

1. No matter where the birth took place, you are likely to succeed with the help of an adoption search and support group, such as one of our affiliates.

2. While Registries do produce results, and you should register with ISRR (Soundex), the odds of succeeding by placing your information in a registry or bulletin board are very much against you.

Any registry that you have to pay for is probably going to rip you off because there will not be the hundreds of thousands of names necessary for a registry to have any chance at all of working.

The same holds true for DNA testing purporting to help you in your search!

The answer to this is Active Searching Pays Off. Most people find who they are looking for with the help of a group.

3. Reunions do NOT fix anything. They can be wonderful, but a reunion is just the beginning of a new way of life and it requires a lot of work to have a successful relationship and have beneficial changes take

place. Someone contemplating a search should try to get in touch with the feelings they have about the person they are seeking, and get in touch with what they want from the person sought and what they want the reunion to do for them.

4. It is very advisable to go to support group meetings (if possible) for at least six months before your reunion. This is minimum preparation for one of the most important events in anyone's life.

5. The search has responsibilities towards the person they are seeking. Sensitivity, Caring and Empathy must rule.

6. Read the <u>Reunion Guidelines</u> in this book.

7. Please read as much adoption related literature as you can.

8. Please try to do your own search as much as possible.

9. Please don't do someone a favor by doing their search as a gift for them. It may backfire and many people can get hurt. Insist that they prepare by doing the work outlined in this appendix.

10. If you have questions about these guidelines, please email me with your concerns.

joesoll@adoptionhealing.com

Appendix E:

Quotable Quotes

"I was born to a woman I never knew and raised by another who took in orphans. I do not know my background, my lineage, my biological or cultural heritage. But when I meet someone new, I treat them with respect... For after all, they could be my people." - James Michener, Author

"The law must be consonant with life. It cannot and should not ignore broad historical currents of history. Mankind is possessed of no greater urge than to try to understand the age-old questions: "Who am I ?", and "Why am I?" Even now the sands and ashes of the continents are being sifted to find where we made our first steps as man. Religions of mankind often include ancestor worship in one way or another. For many the future is blind without sight of the past. Those emotions and anxieties that generate our thirst to know the past are not superficial and whimsical. They are real and they are "good cause" under the law of man and God." - Hon. Wade Weatherford, S. Carolina Circuit Court Judge

"In all of us there is a hunger, narrow and deep, to know our heritage, to know who we are and where we have come from. Without this enriching knowledge, there is a hollow yearning. No matter what our attainments in life, there is a vacuum, an emptiness and a most disquieting loneliness!" - Alex Haley, Author

"The horrors of war pale beside the loss of a mother." - Anna Freud

"The horrors of war pale beside the loss of a child." - Joe Soll

"One of the saddest things of all is that so many adoptees and moms are afraid to take the risk of healing which is necessary to pursue one's dreams" - Anon

"We can evade reality, but we cannot evade the consequences of evading reality." - Ayn Rand

"History is a set of lies agreed upon." - Napoleon Bonaparte

"At the center of your being you have the answer; you know who you are and you know what you want." ~ Lao Tzu.

"That which can be destroyed by the truth, should be." - P C Hodgell

"If you can't wait for your ship to come in, sometimes you have to row out to it." – Greer Garson

"The hardest thing to explain is the glaringly evident which everybody had decided not to see." - Ayn Rand

"The prisoner disintegrated because he could never find out what he was guilty of" - The Trial by Kafka

"The oppressed should rebel, and they will continue to rebel and raise disturbance until their civil rights are fully restored to them and all partial distinctions, exclusions, and incapacitations are removed." -- Thomas Jefferson

"People cannot endure inexplicable worthlessness" - John D. MacDonald

`Not to have knowledge of what happened before you were born is to be condemned to live forever as a child.' - Cicero (c. 106-43 BC)

"There are ex-husbands and ex-wives but there are no ex-moms, ex-dads or ex-children" - Anon

"Adoption Loss is the only trauma in the world where the victims are expected by the whole of society to be grateful" - The Reverend Keith C. Griffith, MBE

"Emotional sickness is avoiding reality at any cost. Emotional health is facing reality at any cost." - M. Scott Peck

"All children behave as well as they are treated" - Jan Hunt, author of - The Natural Child: Parenting From the Heart

"Inner child work is essential. It's the essence of growth as a whole person" - Cheryl Richardson

"The past isn't dead...........It isn't even past" - William Faulkner

"The only way around is through" - Robert Frost

"Only eyes washed by tears can see clearly" - Louis Mann

"The bond between a mother and her child is naturally sacred. It is physical, psychological and spiritual. It is very resilient and very flexible. It can stretch very far - naturally. Any artificial or violent injury to this "stretch" constitutes a serious psychic trauma to both mother and child - for all eternity. This means that children need their mothers and mothers need their children - whether or not a mother is married or unmarried." - Mothers On Trial, The Battle For Children and Custody, by Phyllis Chesler, copyright 1986, 1987

"Never doubt that a small group of thoughtful, committed citizens can change the world; indeed, it is the only thing that ever has".- Margaret Mead

"We shall not cease our explorations, and the end of our exploring will be to arrive back where we started and know the place for the first time" -- T.S. Eliot

"Hold fast to dreams, for if dreams die, life is a broken winged bird that cannot fly." -- Langston Hughes

"Never let your sense of morals get in the way of doing what's right." -- Isaac Asimov

"It's better to regret something you did than something you didn't do" -- Unknown

"I never gave them hell. I just told the truth and they thought it was hell." -- H. Truman

"Everything I did in my life that was worthwhile I caught hell for." -- Chief Justice Earl Warren

"When people ask us how long does it take for something to manifest, we say, "It takes as long as it takes you to release the resistance. Could be 30 years, could be 40 years, could be 50 years, could be a week. Could be tomorrow afternoon." --- Abraham

"Courage is required not only in a person's occasional crucial decision for one's own freedom, but in the little hour-to-hour decisions which place the bricks in the structure of his building of oneself into a person who acts with freedom and responsibility." Rollo May

Owning our story can be hard but not nearly as difficult as spending our lives running from it. Embracing our vulnerabilities is risky but not nearly as dangerous as giving up on love and belonging and joy.. the experiences that make us the most vulnerable. Only when we are brave enough to explore the darkness will we discover the infinite power of our light." - Brene Brown

"What if a caterpillar said she was too busy, tired, unprepared or afraid to change into a butterfly?" - Doreen Virtue

Topher M. Young Says..."Remember, there are no mistakes, only lessons. Love yourself. Trust your choices, and everything is possible."

"The key to independence lies in knowing that at every moment, in very instance, we are creating our life. The more we acknowledge this truth, the more power and freedom we experience.

Rather than blaming ourselves for the things we do not like in our life, we now realize we are manifesting our reality and have the power to change it.

Our life is a reflection of what we believe we deserve. As we deepen our acceptance of and open ourselves to the Infinite love of the universe, a new power flows through us, releasing us from the bondage of our old way of life." - Shakti Gawain

"A meaningful life is not being rich, being popular, being highly educated, or being perfect...

It is about being real, being humble, being able to share ourselves and touch the lives of others....

It is only then that we could have a full, happy and contented life."

By Mar Razalan.

"In a time of universal deceit - telling the truth is a revolutionary act." - George Orwell

Appendix F:

Recommended Readings:

Adoption Related:

Andersen, Robert, *2ⁿᵈ Choice: Growing Up Adopted*
_____, & Tucker, Rhonda, *The Bridge Less Traveled*

Guttman, Jane,   *The Gift Wrapped in Sorrow*

Hughes, Ann,   *Soul Connection*

Lifton, Betty Jean, *Journey of the Adopted Self*
_____, *Lost and Found*
_____, *To Prison With Love*

Musser, Sandra, *I Would Have Searched Forever*
* _____, *To Prison With Love*

Solinger, Rickie, *Wake Up Little Susie:*
_____, *Pregnancy and Power*
_____, *Beggars and Choosers*
_____, *The Abortionist*

Soll, Joe & Buterbaugh, Karen W. *Adoption Healing... a path to recovery for mothers who lost children to adoption*
Verrier, Nancy Newton, *The Primal Wound*
_____, Coming *Home to Self*

Inner Child:

Asper, Kathryn, *Abandoned Child Within*

Bradshaw, John, *Homecoming: Reparenting Your Inner Child*

Ferrucci, Piero, *What We May Be*

Miller, Alice, *Drama of The Gifted Child:*

General:

Bass, Ellen & Davis, Laura, *The Courage to Heal: Guide for Women Survivors of Sexual Abuse*

Chamberlain, David, *Babies Remember Birth*

Edelman, Hope, *Motherless Daughters: The Legacy of Loss*

Estés, Clarissa Pinkola, *Women Who Run With The Wolves*, *The Gift of Story* and *the Faithful Gardner*

Gallagher, Winifred, *I.D.: How Heredity and Experience Make You Who You Are*

Hermann, Judith, *Trauma and Recovery*

McClain & Adamson *The Complete Idiot's Guide to Zen Living*

Neubauer, Peter B. et al., *Nature's Thumbprint: The New Genetics of Personality*

Pearce, Joseph Chilton, *Magical Child*

Verny, Thomas, *Secret Life of the Unborn Child*

114

Part Three

Voices from Exile by Joss Shawyer, concerned citizen.

"The ignorant mind, with all its infinite afflictions,
passions and evils, is rooted in three poisons.
Greed, anger and delusion."- Bodhidhama

Death by Adoption

When my book Death By Adoption was published in New Zealand in 1979, it caused quite a stir. There were many reviews, some supportive, others downright scary, but one that stayed in my memory was printed in a Catholic publication. The reviewer berated me for what was described as my "angry and bitter" stance against adoption, that sacred cow that had always been off limits to criticism. You would have thought that I had burnt the national flag or otherwise committed an act of unforgivable sedition, instead of simply exposing the traffic of adoption for what it was; a wholesale oppression of unmarried women and the children born to us outside of formal marriage.

Five years previously I was asked to address a group of social workers to present my views for single mothers and against adoption. By the time I finished speaking, some of those social workers were on their feet and screaming at me. One even cried real tears as she tried to process what I had said. I could see how very disturbed social workers were as a group and what a vested, very personal interest they had in adoption. But then they were almost like God, really - in the powerful position of giving away other people's children. And of course, they had never been challenged.

But in those days women were not supposed to think or say things that were remotely political. That was the territory of men. Women certainly never told the truth - about their own lives; about unwanted or unplanned pregnancies, about being a battered wife perhaps, or about having been raped. 'Good' women, that is, women that men approved of

116

- were essentially passive women. They kept their mouths shut about the crimes committed against them, and especially about the traumatic life experiences that were the lot of all fertile women. And then, with the advent of women's liberation the entire social climate changed.

It seemed that overnight women were speaking out, rejecting the terrible, damaging passivity that men had enforced in order to maintain gender control for so long. What a relief it was to be a woman who did not give a toss what anyone thought about what she thought, or said. It was a wonderful freedom to be oneself and there would be no going back.

I became one of those outspoken, stroppy feminists tired of being oppressed, in my case because I was a single mother. One who had rejected adoption as an acceptable solution to a pregnancy other people found inconvenient. My experiences of serial oppression perpetrated on me throughout my twin pregnancy gave me the wonderful gift of understanding that the condition of single mothers being oppressed by every man and his passive hand maidens was universal. What had happened to me was happening to all women in the same situation. I began to seek answers. That led me to the obvious starting place; sexism and social policy. I began to research adoption. It gave up so much information, the quest for the truth turned into a book.

People still ask about the title and why I chose it. Here are quotes from the book in explanation as to why the term 'Death By Adoption' summed up the mothers' collective suffering for me, and still does.

"Death by Adoption is the death experienced by the real mother. The baby she carried can actually die for her at either the moment of birth or as she signs consent. It would be more bearable if the child really did die, for then she could grieve and so recover from the death. But although the child died for her, it remains very much alive for someone else. And alive for her too. Or it would be, if it weren't dead. Although some adopted children die in childhood she will never know if one of them is hers and will continue to look in hope (when there is no hope) that one day her child will try to find her. From the moment her child is gone, she must hide the stretch marks and pretend she never had a baby. We do not allow her to grieve and even if we did and she understood why she feels the way she does the grief will always remain unresolved for the simple reason that the child is not dead.

Some women recall vividly both the actual birth and the signing of 'consent'. Although their pain has still not diminished, by allowing themselves to feel the rage and hatred, they somehow found the strength to face it at the time. Some women suppress their pain so successfully that they cannot recall a single detail. They know a child was born and subsequently adopted but cannot recall the date, year and sometimes even the season of the birth. No memory of either hot or cold weather; not a single event connected with the pregnancy or the birth, which is still lying dormant in her mind.

Wanting her opinion on it as a possible dust jacket for this book, I handed the official adoption consent form to a woman who clearly remembered the birth in every detail. Her hands began to shake as she realized what I had so casually placed in them. No recollection of having seen it before. No recollection of signing it. She supposed she must have gone to a lawyer's office, somewhere. For the first time she experienced the loss of her death by adoption. There are an estimated one hundred thousand adopted people in New Zealand. They all had mothers, women who, by being made to believe they had no right to love the babies they carried and birthed, were forced to relinquish all contact.

How many are set free? How many remain trapped inside an emotional nightmare with unresolved grief as a lonely companion. Only humane legislation can ease the pain.

Alas, twenty five years after I wrote those words, the 'humane legislation' that would permit a dual right to search, and also allow a mother of a 'taken' child to have contact with that child as of right throughout its early life, remains on hold.

118

While there have been legal gains to open records in many countries for the adults adopted as infants, to enable them to locate their natural mothers and through them, their fathers, the mothers themselves remain locked into the pain of what is a terrible, irresolvable grief, into reunion and often beyond.

The mothers of the children taken into what is now seen as a form of slavery, whereby an infant is stripped of all its legal rights to identity, including the loss of its entire genealogy through falsified birth records, continue to suffer. Even in reunion, the symptoms of the various psychiatric conditions directly caused by forced adoption haunt the mother whose 'cure' depends on the resilience of herself and her now grown infant, to forge a healthy relationship based on the mutual trust and affection that has been denied them since before the birth itself.

But even in the 'best case scenario' where there is a successfully bonded reunion, those lost years and that lost infant can never be regained. Both are gone forever. This is crazy making stuff for the mother.

There is no doubt that many, many adopted people suffer too - from a lack of identity, from a lack of a feeling of belonging in the 'right' family i.e. their natural family, from a feeling of 'unnaturalness' caused by being in a substitute home, often based on a lack of the attachment that was always supposed to happen according to the trite psychology applied by trite social workers to the children they displaced. It was believed - wrongly - that babies would automatically respond to affection from a stranger. It was also believed - wrongly - that the adopters would feel an automatic attachment to their new acquisitions.

Sadly, the two way attachment process happened far less often than was publicized by social workers covering their tracks, or covering up what they believed to be their own mistakes but were actually just a side product of adoption itself. The inevitability of failed adoption is inherent in the process of attempting to 'attach' people never meant by nature to belong together in the first place, a process destined to fail.

It is well known that when records open the adoption brokers panic. In the mid 1980's, when it became apparent that the New Zealand government would vote legislation to open birth records for adult adopted people, there were rumors of dire action being taken by social workers around the country. For instance, I was told at the time by a reliable source that social workers at a public hospital were keeping busy shredding adoption records.

Social workers were covering their tracks, including their illegal acts. Destroying official records meant breaking the law as well as professional ethics to obliterate records that would reflect badly on themselves. That these were the same people entrusted to place new born infants into sound homes with substitute parents showed us just how flimsy and how dangerous adoption law and practice actually is. It is unsound, unsafe, and totally unjustified.

The mothers of the children kidnapped for adoption during the 'baby scoop' era of thirty to forty years ago, were so damaged by the experience they are only now starting to speak out publicly about the crimes committed against them by the adoption industry and that happened with the full collusion of the state. Adoption has been proven to be a failed social experiment that has left a trail of destruction in its wake.

Stranger adoption should be considered a crime against humanity. It is experienced as an emotional death by the mother who does not recover;"(For) the saddest and most horrifying aspect of adoption is the amount of emotional damage inflicted upon the natural mother. To call her the 'birth mother' instead of the 'natural mother' allows her only the physical birth and denies her those feelings she wasn't supposed to have. By implication this makes the adoptive parents unnatural, but secret adoption cannot be considered natural when the real mother, the victim of this hit and run, is left battered shocked and damaged. Nothing could be more unnatural".

Like everywhere else, stranger adoption North American style can best be described as a 'hit and run', a non-accidental crash site with two

120

primary victims, mother and child. But unlike everywhere else, it is apparent that what drives North American adoption is the money made by the baby brokers, those heinous people and their supporting organisations that traffic in human beings. They buy and sell infants and children. They import and export, just as the original slave traders did. Misery and mental illness are their environmental side products that are polluting the lives of their victims across generations.

One day there will be a reckoning. As North American adoption records open - and it is inevitable that they will open - the truth about adoption law and practice American style will find its way into the public arena. And there seems little doubt that in the future the mothers of all the children forcibly taken for adoption will have their day in court.

It is also entirely probable that the Administration of the United States will finally be forced to offer up a public apology to the hundreds of thousands of American mothers whose children have been redistributed for the purpose of appeasing the right wing faction, that 'moral majority' that is actually a minority, but with a power base far in excess of their actual numbers.

But it is a certainty that a 'third wave' of North American feminist theory will be crafted, defined and taught by the first mothers of adoption slavery, who will lead the 'new woman' in a wave of political action to outlaw stranger adoption and restore families torn apart by domestic slavery.

This third wave of feminism will replace that tired old 'second wave' of feminists who have failed their fertile sisters so badly, so knowingly, so willfully by taking part so willingly in the terrible crimes committed against them; stealing their children away and failing to stop it from happening.

"The revolutionary woman must know her enemies, the doctors, psychiatrists, health visitors, priests, marriage counselors, police-men, magistrates, and genteel reformers, all the authoritarians and dogmatists who flock about her with warnings and advice. She must know her friends, her sisters and seek in their lineaments her own." Germaine Greer, The Female Eunuch. (1971)   -

Touched by Adoption, with a Blowtorch

There is a very coy and popular descriptive term being bandied around the baby breeding industry. It claims to encompass the parties involved in adoption, with the seductive promise that the experience is something to be welcomed. It implies a gentle stroke, a sensitive maneuver, a soft caress. The expression is 'touched by adoption'. Personally I don't think most people whose lives have been derailed by adoption would remember the experience as a mere 'touch'. Most find it a lot more threatening than a gentle pat or a friendly punch on the arm.

Mothers in particular are more likely to experience adoption as a nasty shove, a hostile hit, all the way along the spectrum of psychological violence to a hard bash with a heavy sledgehammer. A crack on the head with a baseball bat. A push into a large pit with very sharp sticks poking out. Or an unpleasant, one way journey to a torture chamber, all expenses paid of course. (Of course!) At the very least, any bereft mother will relate to the touch of adoption as a fearful and very authoritative tap on the shoulder that signifies her time is up, it is time to hand over her baby, time for her to go.

Given that the expression 'touched by adoption' does not reflect the actual adoption experience adequately, it should be renamed. I am delighted to announce a competition with a prize for the winner of the best alternative term that adequately describes the major damage adoption brokers sprinkle around so liberally. I am still musing on what the prize should be, and favor the suggestion made by a natural mother,

123

that the winner should be presented with a small creature, as a suitable replacement for the traditional child often mistakenly adopted in place of a pet. She holds the view that a pet could have an educational value and encourages pre-adopters to enter the competition.

This mother wants to implement a non-human adoption policy whereby pre-adopters are offered alternatives to real live babies and children. When applying to adopt, they would be sent the 'pet' along with accompanying pamphlets describing the importance of allowing their latest acquisition access to social interplay with other members of their own species. Therefore adopters would be encouraged to understand that dogs must be allowed to play with other dogs, and cats allowed access to other members of their feline family and so on.

This process would allow pre-adopters to work slowly towards grasping an understanding of the very difficult concept of 'open adoption' as it pertains to humans and their natural relationships. The huge failure of adopters and their supporting industry to understand the term justifies the implementation of a brand new system designed to educate on it's meaning and practical application.

In the meantime, all human adoptions should be halted, to give pre-adopters time to grapple with these very difficult concepts and internalize them. Given their rate of progress to date, it may take a generation or two before these ideas actually sink in.

To assist in the renaming of the effect the phenomena of stranger adoption has on its victims; that is, the mothers and their children who are less than pleased by the transaction outcomes once they have regained their wits sufficiently to voice their outrage - a process that takes years - here are a few suggestions.

'Torched by adoption' may become an acceptable alternative. Or bashed by adoption, slayed by adoption, enslaved by adoption, disempowered by adoption or maybe just plain old 'kicked in the guts' by adoption. If the last one seems too vulgar, I would be willing to change it to something more delicate, such as 'repressed in the stomach region' by adoption. It does sound nicer, doesn't it? And of course the basic fundamental of adoption is that it is always supposed to be nice. Nice 'waiting families', nice 'unselfish mothers' and 'nice' social workers, doctors and lawyers. And I must not overlook family court judges who are also terribly nice.

Niceness is of course, an aspiration of the middle class, although not much valued by the working class. Just reading this you can very likely tell I was not raised in a nice home at all. You can tell this from my lack of niceness. In spite of this, I happen to know that class plays a major role in adoption.

It is no accident that to be 'touched' by adoption is a phrase coined by the cornerstone of the adoption industry itself - the social work fraternity. It is their transparent attempt to dehumanize their victims through the implementation of minimizing language. It's an old trick of the oppressor. One wonders, do social workers walk or do they run to take part in the separation of mother and baby, not to mention the separation of the baby from all her/his genealogy and natural relationships through the deliberate severing of both maternal and paternal extended family groups.

The middle class dominates the social work profession. It is also the class that most readily volunteers it's daughters as sacrificial offerings when the call goes out for more stock to meet the manufactured and very false demand for new infants. Middle class daughters themselves are raised to be obedient, willing and anxious to please their parents and other authority figures who always know best. Middle class girls are afraid to disappoint and anxious not to offend, all symptoms of the learned helplessness that dominate middle class child rearing techniques. They are raised to require approval, much like Pavlov's dogs. It is a major factor in the signing of consent.

The new adoption term that will replace the very 'feely' 'touched' by adoption could even have a sporty connotation, just for fun. For instance, a mother and her baby could be kicked into adoption, a bit like a rugby ball is kicked into touch. Everyone else on the team just stands around and watches, and cheers when the ball successfully clears the boundary. I do not know what the equivalent play would be in North American football, but the social interaction is the same. And adoption is almost a national sport although without the boundaries and the rules that define other sports. Anything goes in North American adoption. There are no fouls. There is no referee. Funny that the mothers always get sent off!

If you are a victim who has been devastated, brutalized, conned, punched, drugged or otherwise used and abused by the grim practices of North American adoption, then send in your suggestions for a new and vibrant term to replace the misnamed, inadequate 'touched'. The game rules determine that the name must reflect the true horror of adoption upon its victims, mothers and children who were torn away from each other by a money driven industry steeped in corruption and vice. 'Touched' doesn't really cover that, as you see.

North American governments promote the quaint practice of dislocating families and punishing women by continually refusing to provide adequate assistance that would enable them to mother their own children with a semblance of dignity and pride. Remember those politicians when you next go to the polls. It's the least you can do.

Were you marked by adoption? Did you get the tap on the shoulder, calling you to make your personal sacrifice on the bloody alter of patriotic loss? I am sorry to have to tell you, you were had, conned. Had By Adoption. Yes you were. And it isn't nice.

I am hoping that one of my entries including Selected, Tapped, Conned or Socked by Adoption, will take out first prize. I can't wait to claim my brand new frog and make the little darling mine forever. I already have a lovely name picked out to replace the one that his real mother gave him at birth. I even downloaded a birth registration form so I can replace his original correct family information with the made up stuff. I haven't picked his ethnicity yet but I think I favor green.

126

As you have probably guessed by now, I am one of those pre-adopter 'waiting mothers' who really have been 'touched' by adoption in the place where it always seems to have the most powerful effect - the brain. Now I need a little tadpole as a sister for my frog. I will remember to tell both my frog and my tadpole that their mothers' were very, very unselfish for giving them up of their own free will because they loved them and did not want them anymore. Confused and waylaid by adoption? I am. How about you?

When God Stuffs Up

When it is reported that God made a mistake by popping a baby into the wrong 'tummy', the thinking person works out fairly rapidly that God, or someone masquerading as God, is experiencing some issues that probably need addressing. It is more likely that those who claim that God is making this kind of mistake are actually the ones with the issues, and not God herself.

The popular press likes to tell North Americans that when 'God' makes these mistakes it is up to single expectant mothers to right them by giving their baby to 'deserving' people who want them. Now, why didn't I think of that? It's a hell of a marketing idea although you wouldn't expect it to work on anyone over the age of five. But what a great way to make money, brokering such deals! Fixing God's mistakes and getting rich in the process. This really is capitalist utopia, helping God out and making money at the same time. It's a hell of a thing.

This bizarre fantasy of the pro-adoption world that is apparently widespread in the United States and even portrayed on American television as an appropriate 'origins' story to feed to adopted children, led me to ponder very seriously on the mental state of adopters and pre-adopters who actually recite this trash. That they repeat it to 'their' adopted children is scary news indeed. It is a great shift of responsibility to put adoption onto God as if adoption is merely a part of God's great plan for humanity. Yeah, right. Sure it is.

That the media so often perpetuates this unethical garbage is extremely disturbing.

While it may be tempting to think about all the money I could make brokering the sale of other women's babies, I would expect the average American would have the basic understanding that a pregnant woman is not on a level with God in the first place and therefore is not expected to tidy up after God has been so inattentive to her job description, that a baby has actually been carelessly placed in the wrong uterus. It does not take a great intellectual leap to work out that there is a serious credibility issue inherent in this theory even though it may reflect very sloppy work on God's part.

The mother could be expected to know and understand that she could not compete with God by making a solar galaxy in say, 6 or 7 days or thereabouts. So what makes her think she has the authority to fix one of Gods greatest mistakes by rearranging babies and mothers and thereby obscuring their genealogy? Where does this belief originate?

Well, according to aspects of the American press, God has taken to whispering in the ears of young and not so young, very gullible and stressed women with a baby on the way, that she should take pity on some nice people who need a baby due to their own botched encounters with sexually transmitted infection, or are otherwise infertile due to unfortunate lifestyle choices such as smoking and being overweight, two situations that frequently lead to infertility. And on hearing this message from God of course the mother knows she must give her baby to these other very deserving people.

Um.....forgive me if I don't understand that this is the mother who is not experiencing infertility and therefore has not ruined her child bearing equipment, who must sacrifice herself and her infant for the people who.....what was that rationale again? I never get this right!

The social workers and other adoption brokers who actually hand over children to adopters could consider using this belief system or worldview as a yardstick to weed out mentally/emotionally challenged pre-adopters and any descendants they may have, to ensure they get a mark against their name that would make them ineligible to adopt anything other than a flea or a tadpole for the next 150 years.

This would ensure that this particular American psycho-babble would die out along with any genuine genetic deficiencies that may have contributed to the nation's infertility in the first place. It would ensure that there would be no further need for the adoption of human beings at all because the people who want them/get them would no longer be with us. Perhaps infertility itself is actually God's way to eradicate intellectually challenged belief systems. Well, it's just a theory. But I digress.

When the baby is gone we are left with the mother who has displayed an awesome martyrism, a tremendous self-sacrifice, by offering up her new born infant on the euphoria of indecision, acute fear and a lack of social services. Often she agrees to adoption in the later stages of pregnancy before the baby is real to her. She may do it by signing a 'pre-birth' agreement to surrender her child at birth. But to all intents and purposes it appears to the outside world (that is, the real world outside of adoption) that she is willingly taking part in the transaction of selling the child so others can gain.

That the brokers get the considerable amounts of cash extracted from the adopters probably contributes to the American public perception that the mother must be a gullible woman who probably deserves to lose her child to someone who clearly has a bit more upstairs, in the location where United States citizens calculate profit and loss. It's the North American admiration for the dollar, the capacity to make it and the scorn reserved for those who don't as well as those who appear to be giving it away for free, as these mothers do.

I suspect most surrendering mothers have an environmentally induced need for the approval of adults and that they do not see themselves as adults at the time of the pregnancy or adoption. It is only later, after she has awakened from the long sleep of denial that the surrendering mother looks back and begins to understand her state of mind that contributed to the theft of her infant. Consenting to adoption for no valid reason – and displaying "unselfishness" to please other people is not a valid reason - is caused by a type of learned helplessness that has been identified as present in battered wives who keep insisting they 'love' their batterers. They lose all ability to judge the danger they are in and continue to flirt with their own death. They are confused and anxious to please. They believe the battering to be their own fault. They suffer from low self-esteem. They crave the approval of their batterer.

The same thing happens to vulnerable expectant mothers when their family, the state, the community and the press, gang up on them to insist on forced adoption. It's a hostage situation. Victims of hostage aggression are often identified as suffering from Stockholm syndrome, a dependency phenomena that originates from a position of powerlessness or slavery, and that plays havoc with the minds of its victims. Thus the need for approval, learned helplessness and Stockholm Syndrome all come together and play a role in the suppression of birth memories that can and do lie dormant in the mother for many, many years following her apparent collusion in 'consenting' to adoption. She may have signed her name but she has no recall of doing so. That's not consent – that's coercion.

The modern process of breaking the spirit of an expectant mother for the purpose of stealing her infant, reminds me of that old film taken by Hitler's doctors of their own medical experiments, whereby they left a parent locked alone in a room with their baby, but without food or drink. They watched and filmed through a one-way mirror as the adult victim unraveled. It only took a couple of days for the adults to crack completely. In the same way a vulnerable expectant woman is easy pickings for the public and its press. The North American press behaves just like Hitler's doctors, carrying out goulash experiments on defenseless victim mothers, who are unable to fight back or protect themselves. The North American press appears to be in love with adoption. Or maybe in love with the wash of money always associated with slavery?

The surrendering mother gets a great big tick for agreeing to adoption. It's the oppressors' tick of approval. The internalized oppression that leaves her convinced she has no right to parent her own baby, is driven by a national press that is at the forefront of the pro-adoption movement. Writing sappy stories to convince the mother she must sacrifice her baby to prove she is 'unselfish' would be amusing if it were not so sinister.

Bernstein and Woodward, please come back, your country needs you to carry out investigative journalism into the sinister adoption industry of the USA and Canada.

Some mothers who surrendered subsequently front web sites – or claim to - where they forcibly promote and peddle the idea of adoption to other vulnerable women. In my most charitable moments I think this is because of their current victim status as suffering from learned helplessness, Stockholm syndrome, a bottomless need for adult approval, or a combination of all three. Women who lack self esteem do seem to have a bottomless need for the approval of others.

But what these first mothers are finding is that their adoring public is not as adoring as they expected, and even suspect their motives for trying to convince other women to surrender their unborn children. And I must confess that in my most cynical moments - and I have many - I toy with the idea that the adoption industry, known to be worth billions of dollars, is actually the wallet behind this aggressive and very organized marketing campaign for more adoptive stock.

For many surrendering mothers, the craving for approval originates in a deep well of insecurity that cannot be assuaged no matter how much approval she gets, even though taking part in the formal abandonment of her new born infant is a pretty spectacular, not to mention reckless way to gain the approval of others. If the adoption brokers slip her some cash cunningly renamed 'education fees' then at least they have shared some of the profit they made from selling her infant to the emotionally desperate, unstable people who constitute their client group. The American public may even perceive her more kindly if she makes a little money on the side.

When a pregnant woman has no funds, no support and nowhere to live, how attractive it must be to become a martyr instead of an abandoning mother. To be a kind, caring self-sacrificing brave soul, so UNSELFISH that she would deny herself her baby by generously giving it up, is almost saintly behavior. In the process she escapes a grinding poverty, and social ostracism. The college 'scholarship' she may be offered by the brokers may be thankfully accepted as a marker for her sacrifice. I view these financial inducements as a type of headstone, a marker to her pain.

The mother who surrenders may sleepwalk for a long time before waking to the horror of her loss. During the early stages of her long sleep she will believe the hype of her oppressors, that she will grieve and recover and go on to enjoy the happy life that she deserves. It will be some time before she wakes to the unpleasant truth that the grief goes on and on and on.

Sooner or later the mother understands that the 'open' adoption she was lured into was merely a ghastly, insincere game and that the painful hook upon which she finds herself dangling, has become a permanent state of being. The grief the brokers told her would be temporary becomes a life sentence. She may kid herself for a bit longer, that the grief will pass but inevitably she will know that adoption is the wound that does not heal. It is the gift that keeps on giving - depression, shock and pain. It's the scam of scams of the 20th century, and now the 21st.

It makes a mockery of human rights. The American press might like to write about that. Bernstein and Woodward, are you there?

When Infertility Goes Shopping

As most nations outside of the United States are aware, adoption North American style is pretty much a free market, driven by demand, where 'anything goes' for a price. The latest baby breeding plan to be hatched – excuse the pun – by pre-adopters is the purchase of eggs from healthy, supposedly intelligent white women – that is, in the adoption shopping world, the proof of the mother's intelligence is university attendance. Apparently many women university students are willingly selling off their unfertilized eggs in exchange for money to assist them through their studies. If trading one's own potential children for money is considered evidence of intelligence, one wonders why they bother to enroll in 'higher' education in the first place. What type of university actually accepts their enrolments? This is a worry.

In response to this publicized egg selling racket, a group of first mothers, many of whom have devastating, first hand experience of the damage done to their children once lost to adoption and now found, have suggested that this process of baby farming will soon be streamlined to make it more efficient and also more affordable for women to buy and sell each others fertility. They consider infertility has become sort of like the commodity market, where people can buy and sell things that do not actually exist, like next years coffee or tea crop.

Suggestions to further facilitate the free market approach included the idea of fertility sections in supermarkets, where pre-adopters can pick and choose their embryos. If you think adoption is sane, this makes sense. It would make the purchase of others people's gene pool more accessible, more fair. Everyone would be able to purchase potential babies off the shelf. It would be affordable, very democratic. There would be no controls which would give all 'waiting families' a pretty good crack at someone else's family tree, a phenomena to which infertile people believe they have an absolute right.

Just to clarify, a 'waiting family' is a couple of either gender – mixed or otherwise – or even a single person who for reasons of their own infertility or inability to match egg with sperm, look outside their own bodies for a source of children. The 'family' is apparently the family they will become once they procure a child or children with the expert assistance of fertile women. Or men, as the case may be. The 'waiting' sounds passive but actually alludes to the frenetic chase for sperm, eggs or ready hatched children born, or about to be born, to some poor woman without the emotional or financial support to raise her own child. While they 'wait' for someone's else's egg, sperm or personal tragedy to provide them with a 'family' these infertile pre-adopters actively seek the source of their fantasy 'family'. This involves grim chases on internet sites looking for a brokers who will provide them with the opportunity to create a child from scratch or assist them to steal one ready made. They then make the real mother go away so they can pretend they had her child themselves. It's pathetic. It's mad. It should be outlawed.

There is so much nuttiness surrounding adoption throughout the United States and Canada, I think it should be formally considered a form of mental illness. That the adoption insanity has been normalized in the way it has, does not make it sane. Grief literature explains explicitly, the importance of human beings coming to terms with personal loss, in this case, their own lack of fertility. Sound mental health depends upon the ability of individuals to come to terms with their life experiences and regrets.

No matter how personally difficult coming to terms with infertility may be, it is far, far less painful than losing a child to adoption. Women

136

whose children are stolen by this legislated social policy never actually get over it even though all the advertising that supports the adoption industry, says they must. They are stripped of their child and then abandoned to an exile of an emotional wilderness so extremely devastating, it is hard to find words to describe it. I cannot imagine that the 'loss' of potential children – who are only an idea – can come anywhere close to the loss of a real child. One already born, to a real live mother who weeps and bleeds and is left to deal with the aftermath of a dead child gone but not actually dead – well – that is crazy making stuff. That the people who adopt her child do not give a toss about her once the adoption is legalized, illustrates just how little emotional depth they really have. People that shallow don't actually feel hurt deeply. In fact, they should try eating less cheese or stop eating supper altogether before bedtime, as they may be confusing symptoms of indigestion with emotional 'pain'. These things are not the same.

Infertile people need to face their infertility and get over it. They need to weep and cry and scream 'unfair' and then dry their eyes and get on with life. They need to face the fact they are not 'waiting families' but just sad insecure people who need to find outlets for what they imagine are unfulfilled maternal or paternal feelings but may actually be something entirely different. Infertile women need to look outside of other women's families to find fulfillment in their own empty lives. I suspect that most of the trouble over adoption is the inability of infertile women to find meaningful direction in their lives apart from the culturally induced expectation of the supposed happiness that will come from raising a child – any child. There is no inherent 'right' to other people's children. It only exists in the hype of the adoption industry which is a money making business that feeds off its own misinformation, or should I say, bullshit.

As one first mother from the United States commented, "What is normal? Pretty soon I think having your own child will be abnormal, so many other ways to make families, buying, selling, facilitation, buying embryos, sperm..............what is normal?..."

What indeed. The other day I read somewhere that there are an estimated 50,000 fertilised embyos stored on ice around the United States, waiting for their parents to decide the right time for them to be born. If ever. How terrible. How sad. The nation that has everything, with a population that believes it has a right to more of just about anything, may have nothing at all that is actually worth envying apart from central air conditioning and those nifty little plastic bags that come with their own zippers.

Nature vs. Nurture - The Mystery Gene

Almost every pro-adoption publication reports negative behaviors of adopted children and attributes these aberrations to pre-adoption life, and specifically to the natural mother and her family. Or the natural father and his family. This phenomena has been labeled by adopters as the Mystery Gene.

The Mystery Gene is a nasty little fellow that can strike at any time. It is responsible for all kinds of problems in substitute homes. The Gene operates as a sort of malevolent Casper to the adoptive world. Apparently this devious gene somehow manages to escape and inhabit the child before the original birth records can be sealed, thwarting the adopter's best attempt to prevent its appearance. It is hard to pin down, hard to catch, and harder to deny, even when those in closest contact with it, are in denial themselves.

This little rascal, the Nature Gene that unfortunately attaches itself to adopted children, can erupt in bad behaviors without warning. It even has its own language, sort of like a script common to the children it inhabits. The Gene speaks through the adopted child and says things like "you're not my real mother" - or father. It tells children to slam doors and forget to do their homework.

One adopted boy, now an adult, reports that he grew up believing he had inherited a Poor Student Gene that intimidated him in the classroom and hindered his learning. He didn't know why he had so much trouble concentrating on his schoolwork. His adopters solemnly explained to him that he had inherited this Bad Nature Gene from his mother, who was most likely Trailer Park Trash amongst other sins. They seized every opportunity to reinforce their punitive judgment of his mother.

They told him this so often that he began to believe it. This made the Gene mad. It told the boy to behave even worse and so he did. It told him he was No Good, just like his mother who was a slut, a prostitute, a drug addict, and exactly like those Bad Women in the bible who deserved to be punished for their sins. His adoption was her punishment for her shameful behavior.

The boy learned from his adopters that he was the result of the sin of which they spoke and that inside him was this Very Bad Gene known as Bad Blood, which is the colloquial expression of genetically inherited traits. He got madder and madder, but eventually learned to swallow his rage in order to keep the peace in the adoptive household, even though this made him deeply unhappy. But the Bad Gene had finally stopped asking questions which his adopters considered a Good Thing.

This adoptive child-raising technique is called Bringing Up the Mystery Gene with Standards and Values that with enough negative reinforcement, will convert Nature to Nurture within about 18 years. When this grim technique works out well, the adopted person becomes a smug, blaming, self-righteous little prig who sneers at his natural mother, wherein his adopters congratulate themselves on having done a fine job. It means they have won the battle with the Rogue Gene.

An even more desirable conversion is when an adopted child shows positive behaviors and academic gifts. The adopters heave a sigh of relief and warmly welcome the Bad Gene's opposite number, Nurture, which has chased away Nature and left a malleable child in its place. Nurture can show itself in musical, academic or sports talents, according to adopters. Sometimes it manifests as Saintly Behavior, that can be mistaken for approval seeking behavior, but fortunately seldom is - as someone from outside the family may wrongly attribute that approval seeking trait to Nurture. But that seldom happens.

Sometimes Nurture makes terrible mistakes that end with death or injury to the adopted child. This is considered rather unfortunate but is shrugged off as happening in all families, not just adoptive ones. Well, thank goodness for that.

However, when the adoptive person rebels, refusing to accept the definition of themselves or their mother as Bad, it is clear to all that Nature has licked Nurture and the long battle for Decency has been lost. The adopters first clue as to the cause of their problems were things the adopted boy was saying, such as "If I'm adopted, where is my real mother?" and "Why didn't she want me?" - questions like that. They didn't know how to answer which just endorsed the existence of the Bad Gene lurking inside 'their' son. If they had shared the same Gene, they would have known what to say. Actually, if they had shared the same Gene, there would have been no mystery. But they didn't and anything they told him just seemed to make the situation worse. It was therefore quite clear that the Bad Gene came from the Gene Tree of the natural family and not their own. It couldn't have. After all, no one in their family had ever behaved like that.

Gosh, During an adolescent identity crisis the boy stopped learning completely and was subsequently diagnosed with Attention Deficit Disorder (ADD). This was attributed to the drugs and alcohol his mother had no doubt consumed during her pregnancy. The boy was notified of this factual evidence of the Bad Gene that had jumped from his mother into his head and disrupted his learning processes. This sensitive information sharing is known as Christian Love in many adoptive homes. Needless to say the son soon gave up the struggle to learn. Perhaps he realized he had learned quite enough already, which shows just how smart he really is.

This Mystery Gene is a real Trouble Maker. The longer it stays around the worse it gets. It can force a teenager to drive too fast, drink alcohol and use other drugs (just like the boy's mother) and stay out

141

well beyond curfew time. Teeth that don't grow straight and require expensive orthodontic treatment can always be attributed to Nature. Everyone knows that Nurture is not responsible for crooked teeth, although Nurture is responsible for paying the dental bills. Nature gets bad grades and talks back. It can be sullen and resentful when lied to about its origins. Most of all, it can be Ungrateful, which is often the easiest way to identify it. Luckily, adopters are good at spotting it hanging around their home.

But the most reliable way to identify the Mystery Gene is when the adopted child, now grown into a lanky adult - or a short one - who may not resemble his or her adopters, brings home the unwanted news of an unexpected and unplanned pregnancy. The Mystery Gene has surfaced once again. Just like his/her mother, completely irresponsible. Nothing to do with Nurture, especially the adopters lack of responsibility in failing to provide adequate education regarding fertility, as one might expect them to do as a parenting duty. But I suppose that's an occupational hazard of being an adopter - it must be so tempting to forget the potential dangers of fertility associated with Nature, that old Rogue Gene that just won't stay away.

This in-your-face fertility is the worst thing the Rogue Gene can do. The situation frequently ends in yet another adoption, which is the only way to get the Rogue Gene under control. You actually have to breed it out of existence if you want it to shut up. If the purpose of the boy's adoption was to obscure the adopters infertility problem, then the Rogue Gene was really asking for its own obliteration - and so brought its expulsion from this Sacred Adoptive Family Unit upon itself. Entirely.

But what beats me is - how did this boy's mother - this socially, educationally, economically challenged young woman with such incredibly high-risk behaviors, even live long enough to give birth to her son in the first place?. Adopters know for a fact she would have stopped off on the way to the trailer park to shoot up, get drunk, have sex with goodness knows who, then crash the stolen car she was joyriding in, along with her equally worthless friends.

142

And given the poverty status of most first mothers during pregnancy, how they and their families could even afford to support the expensive Bad Habits of that Evil Gene is the Real Mystery. It is perplexing. Social workers, researchers and policy makers should look into this. The Mystery Gene will still be there, waiting to be noticed. I think it's just been trying to get their attention, all along.

The Perpetrators of Adoption Crime

Every crime has at least one victim and one perpetrator and adoption is no different.

Just as in any regular kidnapping, the first victim - the first mother, is taken for a ride, in this case by an organized crime syndicate, overseen by the government and executed by its appointed agents. Adoption victims are told to get lost, made to get lost, banished into exile and rewarded with the approval of professional perpetrators, for keeping their mouths shut about what actually happened. The second victim of adoption is the ransomed baby that is not returned.

Remember Patty Hearst, the famous kidnap victim who was brainwashed by her kidnappers, terrorized and victimized so effectively she came to believe they were her supporters.

By the time she had blasted her way through a few banks, they were her only supporters because no one else could understand the process she had undergone. Whatever made Patty Hearst pick up a gun and assist her kidnappers to rob banks!

Who could possibly relate to that? First mothers can.

They identify with their oppressors, just like Patty Hearst. They have their reality distorted by the perpetrators, all those who gain from adoption crime. Like Patty, adoption victims are temporarily grateful for the approval extended in return for their compliance.

144

Then they come to their senses. By that time, adoption consent is signed and they are in a prison of exile, complete with psychological bars to maintain the threat of 'confidentiality'. Like Patty, they only get that approval when they do what these criminals want them to do - rob the bank, surrender the baby. And like Patty, they need deprogramming afterwards in order to know and understand exactly what happened to them, how they were disempowered by their own overwhelming, situational fear created by their tormentors, who practice a mental form of rape.

Adoption is the only kidnapping in the law books where the perpetrators actually get to keep the ransom. The only way for the mother to protect herself and her baby from the threats of these kidnappers, is to surrender it to them. Guns are not needed - fear of the future is the main weapon used in this crime. It's ridiculously easy to distress and confuse any new mother suffering from an imbalance of hormones following a birth. Like taking candy off a baby, or taking a baby off your victim once you have her vulnerable, confused, depressed, and also desperate for your approval. In rape literature this is known as 'dehumanising' your victim.

When a baby is abducted in public there is a public outcry. The bereft mother is seen on TV, surrounded by grim faced police officers coaching her to beg for the rapid and safe return of her stolen child. Public sympathy is with her. There can be no doubt in the viewer's mind that the mother is a victim every bit as much as the child. Her suffering is apparent. No one questions her anguish. The nation prays for the safe return of the abducted child and rejoice when it happens. This does not happen with adoption crime, which is carried out in private. But by not speaking out against adoption, the public becomes just another category of perpetrator, by default. Or perhaps they are planning to adopt?

Often the public abductor is a woman who is infertile or has suffered the loss of her own child. After being caught and the baby safely restored to the arms of its grateful mother, this perpetrator is offered psychiatric treatment for the previous loss that drove her to such deviant, anti-social behaviour.

But for all the horrified sympathy, there is no doubt in the publics' mind that the kidnapper is quite mad to have done such a thing. She must also be punished, but criminal court judges tend to look upon such crimes with pity, on the premise that anyone driven to such a desperate act as stealing the child of another woman is mentally ill and quite deranged and needs firm correction, tempered with a good dollop of compassion. It is understood that the personal pain of irreversible infertility or child-loss is so damaging that this kidnapper was driven to steal the baby. Clearly, overwhelming personal pain explains this wickedness.

No one doubts the bereft mother has suffered enormously. We identify with her - what loss we ourselves would feel should our precious child be abducted. And in a normal, safe place like a shopping mall, a maternity ward, a bank. But the kidnapper is merely exercising a short cut to stranger adoption, cutting out all the middle men and women, the retailers, those social workers and lawyers and legislators, the adoption brokers, the fences' of these stolen goods. The role of the illegal kidnapper is therefore that of wholesaler to the adoption industry.

The other perpetrators of adoption must also be in some kind of personal pain. This may comprise guilt presenting as denial. Perhaps they too have lost a child or are infertile, and cannot face their grief. Another woman's child becomes the band-aid for their wound. This certainly applies to the receivers of adoption crime. For the other perpetrators it may just be plain old-fashioned greed, that heart-stopping moment at the traffic lights, when they look out of the window of their elderly station wagon and the Porsche is right there, with an engine so quiet you can't even hear it. I can relate to that. And so can the judges in the family courts who bless and bible these transactions of legalized kidnapping. But then all robbers use distributors to shift their stolen property.

The health 'professionals', the adoption social workers, clearly suffer from emotional problems. They understand they were created in the image of God and therefore like to imitate his works. They also have an income issue. They base entire careers on a specialization that includes advancement and salary increments. Imagine if you can, building your own future doing God's work, placing children almost in their own families, with the added benefits of a guaranteed career path with guaranteed advancement, only to realize that what you are doing is wrong.

It's like a person with an overweight problem eating chocolate to deal with the depression they feel when they remember how destructive they are being, opening another box of chocolates to make themselves feel better. If adoption no longer feels good, arrange another one quickly, to push the guilt away. Any surfacing of guilt or regret at swindling defenceless young mothers out of their babies, and all the brainwashing techniques that involves, can only be assuaged by doing another adoption, and another and another. The dynamics of adoption are remarkably similar to drug addicted behaviour. It becomes compulsive behaviour, not to mention repulsive behaviour. Having distanced their 'professional' heads so far from any sense of human decency, adoption social workers become unable to distinguish between right and wrong. They have become amoral, along with their literature.

There is a huge, so-called 'body of knowledge' that has grown up around adoption social work that allays any doubts an individual social worker might have as to the ethics of what she is doing when she arranges an adoption. Yes, of course they write it themselves - silly you!

But social workers come very close to not taking the baby away from the mother - as close as they can get without actually doing it. They 'match' the characteristics of the natural parents with those of the adoptive applicants to ensure that this child is placed as nearly as possible into its own natural family. Matching is promoted on the basis that the child is most likely to be accepted and attach to substitute parents of similar genetic and social aspects to the natural parents, which makes nonsense of adoption at every level. If children are better off in their own families then surely....Silly me, I keep forgetting the money.

Another consideration is that carrying out adoptions creates a feeling better than Prozac, better than religion, better even than late model cars. It gives the perpetrators an adrenalin rush. Better than God. And the receivers are so grateful to the judge, the social worker, and the lawyer. They may even thank the mother nicely, if coolly, for her 'gift' to them before they send her on her way with a couple of letters and an out of focus photograph that won't identify the ransom that they are, astonishingly, allowed to keep.

The perpetrators of adoption may be suffering from psychiatric and social dysfunctions that cause their destructive, compulsive behaviour. Perhaps they are exhibiting a psychiatric condition not yet diagnosed that includes a power need so great they are prepared to destroy the new mother psychologically in order to sell off her child to the highest bidder. But probably there is nothing more to adoption crime than good old-fashioned human greed, just like any old robbery planned and carried out for personal gain, no different to any other criminal doing any other crime. The brokers of adoption, the middle men and women, so empathetic with their clients who pay and pay and pay for the child they believed they wanted, continue to retail this traffic in human babies.

And like all armed robbers on the way to the bank, they prefer not to think about the injuries they are about to inflict. That would get in the way of the money. And that's mostly what North American adoption is about.

If considered at all, the first mothers of stolen children, many of whom now suffer from Post Traumatic Stress Disorder amongst other serious conditions, as a direct result of adoption kidnapping, are seen as just another bank guard who accidentally got in the way. As any armed robber will tell you, they didn't mean to hurt anyone. They just wanted

148

the cash. The gun went off by itself. Funny how they always claim they never touched the trigger.

'Choosing Adoption' – *Adoption Choice* is a Feminist Issue.

The beginning of the adoption quadrangle is the unplanned pregnancy, the single mother-to-be and her choices that are limited, determined by the resources she does not have at her disposal. The most obvious of these is an income and related benefits sufficient to raise a child and also maintain a home, keeping herself and her child in a reasonable standard of living for about 20 years.

If she cannot do this, or cannot see a way to do this, then the so-called 'choice' of whether or not to raise her child herself, does not actually exist. The single mother-to-be then becomes no more than a cog on the production line of a national or international adoption industry that waits like a huge impersonal monster, for the next 'unwanted' baby to roll off the line - at a price. Profit or non-profit, the result is the same for the woman who must lose her child to satisfy the perceived economic 'problem' of her fertility.

Thus the adoption 'triangle' is really a quadrangle because the money aspect of arranged adoptions has now become the cornerstone of evolved adoption law and practice, particularly in Canada and the USA. Adoption is about money and also about punishment of the woman who did have sex without the resources necessary to raise a child, mainly a second wage earner, previously known as a husband. In that famous slogan of feminist politics 'the personal is political'; there is no more political situation for a woman than to find herself trapped in a personal situation whereby her future is about to be determined,

150

dramatically, by her present fertility status. Her 'choices' are determined by her access or lack of access to resources needed for the survival of herself and her infant. Perhaps the most important of these is the personal resource of self-esteem, a powerful belief in herself sufficient to withstand the disapproval of family, friends and society in general, a belief strong enough to enable her to strike out into a parenthood, alone.

The unbearable suffering of women who have lost children to adoption is currently being documented. Reunion organizations around the world are growing in strength, and sealed adoption records are under political pressure from women no longer prepared to always be the losers in the failed social experiment that is stranger adoption. Mothers are searching for their children - children are searching for their mothers - and fathers. Many are successful and can testify to the loss of identity, the rage and the bottomless grief that adoption introduced to their lives.

But where do feminists stand in this tangle of forged birth records, this pseudo-choice of adoption that is actually no choice at all?. During the 'second wave' of feminism that happened in the 1970's in New Zealand, I took a stand for all single mothers including myself. At the time there was a commonly used expression for the rare event of a woman refusing adoption - she was described as 'keeping' her baby. The pretence of 'choice' was even then well entrenched in the language of adoption and single pregnancy in spite of the reality of a rare and very limited choice that resulted in the vast majority of babies born to single mothers being adopted to strangers.

Yes, a single woman could 'keep' her baby if she could overcome widespread social disapproval, abject poverty with poor housing, associated poor health, an absence of any personal or financial support and somehow maintain enough self esteem to see her through whatever lay ahead; usually more of the same. It was a daunting 'choice'. It was a farce.

However, with the feminist revival women's fertility was correctly identified as the core cause of gender inequality. If women could control their fertility, the power relations between men and women would change and all women would benefit. Sisterhood was powerful indeed. Education and related career opportunities became available to women who embraced the resulting lifestyle changes. Fertility -and related marriage or less formal partnerships- could be postponed and even put off indefinitely. This truly was choice for the first time, and women, worldwide, embraced the economic chances for gender equality that fertility control had brought.

And then came a previously unseen problem for many of those women who had postponed their fertility too long, a resulting infertility that could not be reversed. Many decided too late, they wanted a child, or children. Where then, do they look for a solution to this regret; a completion of their lives by the addition of a child?. Adoption.

Does the woman who decides to resolve her infertility by adopting really manage to kid herself that the donor of an adoptable child has a 'choice'?. Would any woman with a choice put herself through nine months of pregnancy and go into labor having made the decision to surrender her child, if in fact there was another way? With the rare exception of surrogacy, carried out for money, no woman would knowingly, willingly do this. Does the infertile woman have the moral right to complete her family with another woman's child? I think not.

Whatever happened to sisterhood, that brave frontier of gender equality where women banded together to fight the monster, that oppressor enabled by a structural inequality that collectively used woman's fertility to keep her oppressed, uneducated, downtrodden, poor. I put it to every woman, that any woman who expects to exercise a 'choice' to fulfill her maternal needs with another woman's child, has herself become that oppressor.

Adoption is the last resort for fertile women too young, too poor, too oppressed to have fertility choices; women lacking in self-esteem, in societal support, and in a belief of themselves. They come from all

152

ethnicities, all cultures, all countries. The woman without choices - surrendering her child for adoption in 2003 - is actually the woman every woman could have been, had the feminist revolution not happened.

Until every woman, everywhere, has the right to raise the child she carried and birthed, the patriarchy is alive and well, still using 'good' women to punish 'bad' women - through the role of adoptive applicant. The personal remains political; adoption is a feminist issue.

Part One

Losing One's Country

Strangers in a Strange Land.

"I want to share with you my understanding of a sacred word, Motherland, to express my perception of its priceless nature and the point of my love for it. These notions have settled down in my soul forever and got a foothold in it."
– Anon

"Motherland is all your dimensions. Motherland will shape your size, weight and color. If sky is your Motherland, you are destined to fly; if the Garagum desert is your Motherland, you will walk on the ground; if mountains are your Motherland, you will climb up and down, if sea is your Motherland, you will swim." – Anon

If you learn to worship your Motherland, you will find a place in your heart for it. Magnificent mountains, clean rivers and the vast of desert, home cities and villages - all of them will have its place in your soul. And then a heart will take a shape of Motherland. You will not be small, you will be big and you will not be a part but a solid body." - Anon

There are hundreds of thousands of adoptees who were born in other countries and brought to strange lands to be with their adoptive families.

They usually arrived in their new countries with the rudiments of their mother tongue already learned. They almost always were new parents who had no knowledge of the native tongue of their new ward.

Therefore they had no way to communicate with the child and the child had no way to understand what was happening to her.

Take any individual adoptee, for example. She could not understand what had happened to her and was happening to her in her new home.

She was surely terrified. She had suffered the horrible trauma of losing her mother, and the additional trauma of being whisked away by strangers to a strange land.

And she has no way of communicating with her new family.

It is highly likely that she will be with a Caucasian family and if her skin is a different color, it is highly likely that she will be bombarded with racist insults, teased for looking different, teased for being adopted. It is highly likely that she will be given an American name which will cause more teasing. It is possible that she will become a house slave, free labor for their new family.

Sadly, it is highly likely that she will be abused in all possible ways. The percentage of foreign born adoptees who are sexually abused is staggering, particularly among female adoptees born in Asian.

It is likely that her new family will be dysfunctional.

It is likely that she will be told she was abandoned which is often a huge untruth.

It is likely that a search for her roots will be extremely difficult. It is likely that she will never meet her family.

What has she lost?

She has lost her mother, her country, her language, her culture. The smells of the air of her country, the smells of her native food cooking, the sounds of her language, the sounds of her music, the look of her own clan, the comfort of being with her own clan, and the list goes on.

She has lost everything dear and the trauma is incalculable.

She has lost people with whom she can communicate.

She has no support, no one who understands and the likelihood is that she will numb out from the pain, fit in with her strange surroundings and perhaps lose conscious awareness of the calamity that has occurred.

The brutal trauma of losing her mom, a trauma worse than the horrors of war, will be added to by the trauma of all the other losses described above. Her trauma can be healed if she finds her inner strength. Her inner strength is in her genes. It is there, she just has to discover it.

I pray that each foreign born adoptee finds that strength and finds peace.

Blessing of Guadalupe

Our Lady of Guadalupe, also known as the Virgin of Guadalupe is a celebrated Roman Catholic icon of the Virgin Mary.

Have you forgotten?
I am your mother.
You are not alone.
You are under my protection.
Anything you need,
Ask me.
Do not worry about anything,
Am I not here-
I who am your mother?
Have you forgotten?
I love you, and
You are under my protection.

Clarissa Pinkola Estés, Ph.D.

About the Author

Joe Soll is an adoptee, author, psychotherapist and lecturer internationally recognized as an expert in adoption related issues. He is director and co-founder of **Adoption Healing (formerly Adoption Crossroads)** in New York City, a non-profit organization that helps reunite and gives support to adoptees, natural parents and adoptive parents. **Adoption Healing** is affiliated with more than 475 adoption agencies, mental health institutions and adoption search and support groups in eight countries, representing more than 500,000 individuals whose lives have been affected by adoption. **Adoption Healing** is also dedicated to educating the public about adoption issues, preserving families and reforming current adoption practices.

The director and founder of the **Adoption Counseling Center** in New York City, Mr. Soll was also co-organizer and co-chair of the **New York State Adoption Agency Task Force**; a member of Matilda Cuomo's 1993 **Advisory Council on the "Adoption Option"**; three time conference chair and board member of the **American Adoption Congress**, a former trustee of the **International Soundex Reunion Registry**, and a former advisor to the **Center for Family Connections**. He is a fellow of the **American Orthopsychiatric Association,** the **National Association of Social Workers**, and a former adjunct professor of social work at Fordham University Graduate School of Social Service.

Since 1989, Mr. Soll has organized and coordinated nine international mental health conferences on adoption for mental health professionals and those affected by adoption. He has been an expert witness in court about adoption related issues and has lectured widely at adoption agencies, social work schools, mental health facilities and mental health conferences in the U.S. and Canada.

Mr. Soll has appeared on radio and television more than 300 times, given more than 150 lectures on adoption related issues and has been featured or quoted in more than three dozen newspapers, books and magazines. In 1994 he was portrayed as a therapist in a NBC made-for-TV movie about adoption,. He played himself in the HBO original movie *Reno Finds Her Mom*. He was featured in the 2001 Telly Award winning Global Japan documentary, "Adoption Therapist: Joe Soll." He has recently been featured in the documentary, "Blood Lines" and profiled in the International Museum of Women. His own story as an adoptee has been presented more than three dozen times on Unsolved Mysteries. He has walked the 250 miles from New York City to Washington, D.C. six times to create public awareness of the need for adoption reform. He resides in Congers, NY and maintains an office in New York City.

www.ingramcontent.com/pod-product-compliance
Lightning Source LLC
Chambersburg PA
CBHW052046090426
42739CB00010B/2064